The Gospel
According
to Dr. Seuss

The Gospel According to Dr. Seuss

James W. Kemp

Judson Press ■ Valley Forge, PA

THE GOSPEL ACCORDING TO DR. SEUSS
Snitches, Sneetches, and Other Creachas

Bible quotations in this volume are from the New Revised Standard Version of the Bible, copyright ©1989 by the Division of Christian Education of the National Council of the Churches of Christ in the United States of America. Used by permission. All rights reserved.

Judson Press and author James W. Kemp express their gratitude to International Creative Management and to Random House, Inc. for making it possible to use excerpts from Dr. Seuss's stories. The books quoted herein are listed below, in order of appearance, along with the credit lines requested by Random House.

HORTON HATCHES THE EGG by Dr. Seuss, copyright TM & copyright © by Dr. Seuss Enterprises, L.P. 1940, renewed 1968. Used by permission of Random House Children's Books, a division of Random House, Inc.

YERTLE THE TURTLE AND OTHER STORIES by Dr. Seuss, copyright TM & copyright © by Dr. Seuss Enterprises, L.P. 1950, 1951, 1958, renewed 1977, 1979, 1986. Used by permission of Random House Children's Books, a division of Random House, Inc.

WHAT WAS I SCARED OF? by Dr. Seuss, copyright TM & copyright © by Dr. Seuss Enterprises, L.P. 1961, renewed 1989. Used by permission of Random House Children's Books, a division of Random House, Inc.

THE CAT IN THE HAT COMES BACK by Dr. Seuss, copyright TM & copyright © by Dr. Seuss Enterprises, L.P. 1958, renewed 1986. Used by per-mission of Random House Children's Books, a division of Random House, Inc.

"The Zax": from THE SNEETCHES AND OTHER STORIES by Dr. Seuss, copyright TM & copyright © by Dr. Seuss Enterprises, L.P. 1953, 1954, 1961, renewed 1989. Used by permission of Random House Children's Books, a division of Random House, Inc.

Library of Congress Cataloging-in-Publication Data

Kemp, James W.
    The Gospel according to Dr. Seuss : snitches, sneeches, and other creachas / James W. Kemp.
        p. cm.
    ISBN 0-8170-1457-8 (alk. paper)
    1. Christian life. 2. Seuss, Dr. I. Title.

BV4501.3.K45 2004
242—dc22

2003070040

Printed in the U.S.A.

12 11 10 09 08 07 06 05 04

10 9 8 7 6 5 4 3 2

To my grandchildren.

May they go beyond zebra in faith and deed.

I thank Randy Frame at Judson Press for his invaluable assistance. He contributed much to this book. I offer my sincere appreciation also to the other members of the Judson Press team for their careful editing (Bob Maccini, Victoria McGoey, and Rebecca Irwin-Diehl) and design (Wendy Ronga).

Barbara A. Kemp, my devoted wife, was one of the few people to give an honest critique of the sermons from which many of these reflections emerged. I am grateful for her love and encouragement. Helen Kemp, my mother and secretary, was a tireless worker and constant encourager. James D. Kemp, my father, assisted with the editing, and Frances Johnson and Barbara Mabry made helpful suggestions.

I thank the congregations I served who first heard Dr. Seuss illustrations in my sermons. These dear friends encouraged me in my pastoral ministry, and they now encourage me in my writing.

Finally, I am grateful to the good people at International Creative Management for allowing the use of material from Dr. Seuss's books.

When I was in seminary, I was asked in a survey about my favorite theologian. Most people answered Karl Barth or Søren Kierkegaard or John Wesley. My favorite theologian was Theodor S. Geisel, also known as Dr. Seuss.

In fact, more than two decades later, Dr. Seuss remains my favorite theologian. When I was a pastor, I found that I could find no better illustrations for biblical principles than I found in Dr. Seuss's stories. His themes help us to understand what is truly important in life. His messages cause us to think about ourselves in new ways.

I preached sermons based on Bible passages, and I used Dr. Seuss to address themes such as faithfulness, fairness, friendship, greed, pride, hope, adventure, and much much more. I hope readers will find in these reflections ideas that can bring relevance to parallel themes found in the Bible. And I hope you will have as much fun reading about cats in hats, Grinches, Snitches, Sneetches, and other creachas as I have found thinking and writing about them.

May the words of my mouth and the meditations of all our hearts be acceptable in God's sight, for God is our strength and our redeemer.

CHAPTER 1

Horton Hatches the Egg

Blessed be the God and Father of our Lord Jesus Christ! By his great mercy he has given us a new birth into a living hope through the resurrection of Jesus Christ from the dead, and into an inheritance that is imperishable, undefiled, and unfading, kept in heaven for you, who are being protected by the power of God through faith for a salvation ready to be revealed in the last time. In this you rejoice, even if now for a little while you have had to suffer various trials, so that the genuineness of your faith—being more precious than gold that, though perishable, is tested by fire—may be found to result in praise and glory and honor when Jesus Christ is revealed. (1 Peter 1:3-7)

And then came the Winter…the snow and the sleet!
And icicles hung
From his trunk and his feet.
But Horton kept sitting, and said with a sneeze,
"I'll *stay* on this egg and I *won't* let it freeze.
I meant what I said

1

And I said what I meant....
An elephant's faithful
One hundred per cent!"

Dr. Seuss's *Horton Hatches the Egg* ranks near the top of the list of books that have made the greatest impact on my life. It is the first book I remember reading or having been read to me. As a child, I showed up every two weeks or so at the Lexington Public Library or bookmobile to check out or renew this priceless volume. Under my mother's careful scrutiny, I would look at the other books in the Kiddies Corner, but inevitably I settled on *Horton* every time. I'd carry it home and crawl into Dad's lap, and then we would go over this rhyming fantasy yet another time.

Horton Hatches the Egg is the story of a kindhearted elephant named Horton, who warms the nest of the lazy bird Mayzie, who talks the unsuspecting elephant into sitting on her egg so she can take a vacation, a vacation that turns into a permanent departure. The elephant promises to fulfill this duty. In fact, nothing can keep Horton from carrying out his mission. Autumn turns to winter, but Horton keeps his post despite the freezing cold. When spring arrives, his animal "friends" show up to make fun of the sight of an elephant sitting in a tree.

Three hunters decide to capture Horton. They take him, tree and all, to make him part of a traveling circus, thinking of nothing but the money they can make from Horton. Horton bears it all, refusing to budge from the egg. In the face of challenges, persecution, and ridicule, Horton remains faithful "one hundred per cent."

The book of 1 Peter was written to the Hortons of the world—that is, faithful people who were living in the face of persecution. The persecution may have been sanctioned by the dictator Nero or perhaps by Domitian, another ruthless leader. More probably it was an unofficial kind of persecution, having arisen from an informal base of hatred, misunderstanding, and resistance to change. The persecution, which was widespread and brutal, was aimed at a people who no longer followed the party line. It was aimed at a minority that refused to conform to the cultic, the moral, the ethical norms and standards of the society in which they lived. These were a different sort of people because they were given a new birth into a living hope through the resurrection of Jesus Christ from the dead.

The book of 1 Peter contains words of encouragement, consolation, and exhortation, declaring toward the end of its final chapter that "this is the true grace of God" and urging followers of the gospel to "stand fast in it" (1 Peter 5:12). It was encouragement in a time of testing.

What was good news for these early followers of Christ is good news for us today as well. It could be argued that the most basic challenge of our practice of faith is to remain faithful, to remain true to our convictions and commitments even when doing so leads to frustration or pain or embarrassment—that is, even when it leads to persecution.

We live in violent and uncertain times, times in which our faith that God is ultimately in control is tested, times when many of the Bible's principles are routinely ridiculed or ignored by our overwhelmingly secular society, times when standing true is a stiff challenge, as it was for Horton. We face tests that, though they may ultimately purify our faith as a refiner's fire purifies precious metal, are wearing us down.

Often the challenges to our faith come in subtle, unexpected ways. My first field education assignment during my seminary years included a hidden test. I didn't know how badly I was failing this hidden test until just a few weeks before the assignment ended. I received a curious sort of compliment that tipped me off that something was seriously wrong. The "compliment" sounded something like this: "We have enjoyed having you with us, Jim. You fit in real well. We were afraid we might get some kind of radical or something. But you haven't upset people by pushing your feelings on racial issues or women's rights and things."

These words stung. In striving to "fit in"—to meet the community's expectations that I not make any waves—I was no longer responding faithfully to the renewing mercy of God. Not long after this, I read Martin Luther King Jr.'s book *Why We Can't Wait,* chapter five of which is his well-known "Letter from Birmingham Jail." He was addressing those who claimed to be faithful clergy but who supported a policy of "moderation," and who thus publicly opposed the Birmingham sit-ins and marches of the spring of 1963. King pointed out that it is not always the KKK or some other blatantly oppressive group that stands in the way of freedom and justice. Often it is the moderates who stand in the way, the so-called faithful who profess concern and commitment but who maintain that the time is not yet right for justice. They are people who insist on waiting for the proper season, but people under whose guidance the right time and the proper season never seem to arrive.

King wrote, "Shallow understanding from people of good will is more frustrating than absolute misunderstanding from people of ill will. Lukewarm acceptance is much more bewildering than outright rejection." Moderation can be deceptive. In fact, lukewarm faithfulness may not be faithfulness at all. If we, like Horton, are to remain faithful, we must be prepared not only to endure ridicule, but also to take action when the cause is right and just, even sometimes when our reputations, safety, and comfort level are at risk.

Let me be quick to add, however, that to endure hardship or persecution is not necessarily a sign of genuine faithfulness. Many a minister has been quick to become a self-declared martyr for a passing cause because, ironically, there is some degree of comfort that comes from being persecuted. It is easy to assure ourselves that because we endure persecution, we are the truly faithful ones. We rally to uphold the banner of righteousness, the cause of the oppressed. We take our stand against the evil forces of this world and confront the enemy boldly with our minds, our hearts, our bodies, and our souls. This is all well and good until this banner becomes a decoration for our reputation, until that defiant stance functions mainly as a platform for self-exaltation. We would be martyrs, glorious martyrs, in the guise of faithful servants. As T. S. Eliot warned, "The last temptation is the greatest treason: to do the right deed for the wrong reason."

The path of genuine faithfulness is long and often lonely. We need Peter's encouragement, especially since our lives often take surprising, unexpected twists and turns. The stories of William Sydney Porter, known and loved as O. Henry, in a way serve as metaphors for life. *The Gift of the Magi, The Ransom of Red Chief, The Cop and the Anthem,* and *The Last Leaf* are but a few examples of O. Henry's stories, which are known for their trademark endings, featuring an unexpected twist. The penniless man tries to get arrested so he can spend the winter in a warm jail cell. Unsuccessful, he resolves to go straight and is promptly arrested for loitering and given three months. The last ivy leaf on the wall turns out to be artificial, painted by an aging artist to preserve the hope of a sickly young girl. Time and time again O. Henry breaks through the reader's expectations to provide surprise conclusions, unexpected twists.

This is exactly what we encounter in the biblical revelation. Again and again in a time of despair or in the midst of persecution, our great God breaks through in unexpected places, producing a triumphant twist that gives us the assurance of victory, the strength for perseverance, the guide for faithful obedience.

In their old age, facing an heirless death, Abraham and Sarah are met by the triumphant twist: a child named Isaac, "laughter," is born! Caught between the water and Pharaoh's charging troops, the children of Israel encounter a triumphant twist as the waters roll back and they pass into freedom unharmed. Even the tale of Job, an innocent sufferer, is confounded by such twists.

It is in these and other biblical accounts that we find true ground for our faithfulness and future hope. The word from 1 Peter to those under persecution—remain faithful—is our word today. After all, the story of God's revelation in Jesus Christ does not end on the cross, but has a triumphant twist, one that "has given us a new birth into a living hope through the resurrection of Jesus Christ from the dead" (1 Peter 1:3). Peter continues, "In this you rejoice, even if now for a little while you have had to suffer various trials, so that the genuineness of your faith—being more precious than gold that, though perishable, is tested by fire—may be found to result in praise and glory and honor when Jesus Christ is revealed" (1:6-7).

This is the good news: our God acted, our God is acting, and our God will act in times to come. It is the triumphant twist of the continuing revelation of God that there is indeed a reason to live faithfully, trusting not in ourselves but in the great mercy that makes us new.

At the end of Horton's story, the lazy bird discovers Horton at the circus and wants to reclaim the egg, even though Horton has kept it warm for fifty-one weeks. In all the commotion, the egg hatches. Out comes not a bird, but a small elephant with wings, a sort of baby Horton. Our God is faithful—"one hundred per cent!" And when we, like Horton, remain true to our word, faithful to the end, we too shall reap our reward.

CHAPTER 2

Yertle the Turtle

When Jesus saw the crowds, he went up the mountain; and after he sat down, his disciples came to him. Then he began to speak, and taught them, saying:

"Blessed are the poor in spirit, for theirs is the kingdom of heaven.

"Blessed are those who mourn, for they will be comforted.

"Blessed are the meek, for they will inherit the earth.

"Blessed are those who hunger and thirst for righteousness, for they will be filled.

"Blessed are the merciful, for they will receive mercy.

"Blessed are the pure in heart, for they will see God.

"Blessed are the peacemakers, for they will be called children of God.

"Blessed are those who are persecuted for right-eousness' sake, for theirs is the kingdom of heaven.

"Blessed are you when people revile you and

persecute you and utter all kinds of evil against you falsely on my account. Rejoice and be glad, for your reward is great in heaven, for in the same way they persecuted the prophets who were before you." (Matthew 5:1-12)

"Everyone then who hears these words of mine and acts on them will be like a wise man who built his house on rock. The rain fell, the floods came, and the winds blew and beat on that house, but it did not fall, because it had been founded on rock. And everyone who hears these words of mine and does not act on them will be like a foolish man who built his house on sand. The rain fell, and the floods came, and the winds blew and beat against that house, and it fell—and great was its fall!" (Matthew 7:24-27)

Yertle the Turtle is the story of a turtle who somehow got the idea that he was king of all he could see. But Yertle the Turtle had a problem. He couldn't see very far. His throne, a mere stone in the pond, was too low. And so King Yertle decided one day to expand his kingdom:

> He sat on a rock and could see all the pond,
> But Yertle could not see the places beyond…
> So, he ordered nine turtles to swim to his stone,
> And using these turtles he built a new throne.

The turtles built this throne by climbing on top of one another. Yertle, of course, got to be on top. On the one hand, it would seem that the higher up Yertle got, the more content he would be. At one point he was high enough to see for a mile, which meant that he was now the ruler not just of his little pond, but also of a cow, a mule, a house, a blueberry bush, and a cat. But instead of getting more content as he got higher, Yertle became less and less satisfied. In fact, the more he could see, the more he wanted to see, and the more turtles he ordered to stack one on top of another underneath him—until...

> That plain little turtle below in the stack,
> That plain little turtle whose name was just Mack,
> Decided he'd taken enough. And he had.
> And that plain little lad got a little bit mad.
> And that plain little Mack did a plain little thing:
> *He burped!* And his burp shook the throne of the king.

Down came Yertle the Turtle, smack into the pond. His new title was "King of the Mud." The story of King Yertle should remind us all of the foolish man, about whom Jesus told, who built his house on the sand instead of on the rock. Yertle had a fall because he failed to build his throne on a solid foundation. Turtle backs are not a very strong foundation for the throne of the king. So weak they were that it took only a little burp to bring down the throne.

Nor did the motivation behind the building of a new throne rest on a solid foundation. Yertle was driven by greed and selfishness, by the desire for more. He wanted to get higher and higher so that he could have more and more power and control. And despite a few passing moments of exaltation, he ultimately—and in fairly short order—came down with a crash.

Each day we have choices regarding how we want the foundations of our lives to look and how solid we want them to be. We can build on values such as greed and selfishness. We can be apathetic by ignoring the human need that surrounds us. Or we can build on the values and principles set forth in Scripture by the Lord of our lives.

As we saw in Matthew 7:24-27, Jesus' words comprise the solid foundation on which we can safely and securely build. Those who seek out Christ's words and obey them are like the wise builder who put his house on a rock foundation so that it would be strong enough to withstand the storms and floods that came along. People who ignore Jesus' words in favor of their own values are building their houses—building their lives—on sand. When we do so, we are at risk of being toppled, Yertle-like, by even the mildest of storms that may come along.

The admonition not to build on sand is found in Matthew's Gospel as part of the most important sermon ever delivered: Jesus' Sermon on the Mount. This sermon includes the Beatitudes, in which we encounter the rocks—the firm foundation—on which to build our lives.

"Blessed are the meek, for they will inherit the earth" (Matthew 5:5). Many associate the word "meek" with being passive, shy, perhaps even a doormat—someone who always gives in to another's will. The biblical concept of meekness has more to do with humility, with seeing ourselves truly, as being no better or worse than we are.

The question of who we are in God's eyes brings to mind another children's story, a story about a land where everybody, including the butcher, the baker, and the candlestick maker, wore a crown. One day a traveler came into this country. This traveler was a photographer who made his living by taking pictures of the royal families. He would take his camera into a country and take a picture of everyone wearing crowns. Then he would put them in an album and sell them to the king of the country for a healthy price.

The traveling photographer set up his camera and started taking pictures in the land where everyone wore a crown. Person after person—man, woman, and child—walked by and, since they all wore crowns, the photographer snapped his camera for everyone. He was busy all day and on into the night. "How could it be?" he wondered. "How could so many people be part of the royal family?"

And so he began asking questions. "Excuse me, Mister Butcher-with-the-Crown. What relation do you have to the king?" "I'm one of his children," the butcher replied, "so I guess I am a prince."

The photographer asked the baker, "Excuse me, ma'am. How are you related to the king?" She answered, "I'm one of his children, a princess." In fact, everyone he met was either a prince or a princess (or at least they claimed to be).

Finally, he had used up all his film, so he headed to the castle with an album full of photos. He knocked at the door, only to be greeted by another man wearing a large crown. "You must be the king," the photographer said. "No, I am one of the king's helpers. I'm also a prince."

"Another prince!" The photographer was amazed. "Tell me, prince, how can there be so many crowns? How can everybody be a prince or a princess? Doesn't it make the king quite mad that everyone is wearing a crown?"

"Mister Photographer," the king's helper replied, "there is a crown here for you, too, if you want it. The king issued a royal decree that everyone who enters this land becomes a member of his family. Everyone here is allowed to wear a crown. Everyone here is a prince or princess. But there is one rule in order to wear a crown: we must remember that he is the king. Here's some more film. Take everybody's picture. We all belong to the king's family!"

The lesson here for children and adults alike is that to be meek means to understand accurately our identity as human beings. This means recognizing that God calls all of us to be his children. We are all princes and princesses in the kingdom of God. But we must always remember that God is the King. Meekness—humility—requires that we always remember that God is the head of the royal family.

Another of the Beatitudes states, "Blessed are those who hunger and thirst for righteousness, for they will be filled" (Matthew 5:6).

Sometimes God requires more of us than we require of ourselves. But let us not forget those times when we require more (or perhaps something different) of ourselves than God requires of us.

Freddy wanted to be a baseball player. He wanted to play for the Reds or the Yankees. Every day he practiced. He threw and threw and threw. He hit and hit and hit. He ran and ran and ran. Freddy wore baseball shirts and a baseball cap, and he had a fine glove and bat. He collected baseball cards, watched baseball games, and even had baseball curtains hanging in his room. Freddy wanted more than anything to be a big-league player.

Freddy played in Little League. And he was pretty good his first year. In his second year he made the all-stars. He grew older and played in the Babe Ruth League and joined his high school team. Freddy kept getting better and better. He was a good ball player, but he still had a way to go to get to the big leagues. However, there was a problem. Freddy kept getting better, but so did everyone else. High school players were a lot better than the Little League players were. Freddy was good, but he was not an all-star at the high school level.

Freddy graduated from high school, but no one gave him a college scholarship. He went to a Reds tryout camp and survived the first cut, only to be turned away the second time. He tried again, but he never made the team.

Finally someone said to him, "Fred, you're pretty good. You're probably as good as you'll ever be, but you don't quite have what it takes to be a major leaguer. Your body is just not built for baseball. You gave it a good try, but perhaps you had better try something else."

Not everyone can be a big-league player. Freddy couldn't have his heart's desire. But what God desired of Freddy has always been available to him. Thank heaven, God's kingdom isn't like baseball. Anyone who wants to play has a place on God's team. Pleasing God ought to be the most important thing in our lives. Jesus cited two fundamental commandments for those who desire to please God. The first is to love God with all our heart, mind, and soul, and the second is to love our neighbor as ourselves. Big-league Christians practice these each day.

Here is one more rock from the Sermon on the Mount:

> "You are the light of the world. A city built on a hill cannot be hid. No one after lighting a lamp puts it under the bushel basket, but on the lampstand, and it gives light to all in the house. In the same way, let your light shine before others, so that they may see your good works and give glory to your Father in heaven." (Matthew 5:14-16)

Yertle the Turtle's light didn't shine very much. In fact, his light shone only on himself. He cared about the other turtles only to the extent that they could serve him, and he landed in mud as a result.

Friends, let us all build on the rock. With apologies to Dr. Seuss, we might say,

Turtles are toppled by mere burps and by sneezes,
But Christ's rock stands firm in all storms and breezes.

We have a rock foundation in Jesus Christ and in the words
and principles he taught us to live by. We build on this foundation by remembering the example of Yertle the Turtle and then
doing the opposite. We build on this rock foundation by recognizing that we are all children of the great King of the universe.
We build by being caring instead of selfish, by pursuing justice
instead of power. We build by letting the light of love for others
shine far and wide.

Chapter 3

What Was I Scared Of?

Then Jesus went with them to a place called Gethsemane; and he said to his disciples, "Sit here while I go over there and pray." He took with him Peter and the two sons of Zebedee, and began to be grieved and agitated. Then he said to them, "I am deeply grieved, even to death; remain here, and stay awake with me." And going a little farther, he threw himself on the ground and prayed, "My Father, if it is possible, let this cup pass from me; yet not what I want but what you want." (Matthew 26:36-39)

For most people, the most uncomfortable human emotion of all is fear. From the time we were children, we have had fears. Most children are afraid of the dark. Some fear being left alone. Many are afraid of snakes and spiders. Some are afraid of animals of any kind, even cute and cuddly puppies.

Perhaps the hardest childhood fear of all to address is the fear of the bogeyman. Because nobody really knows exactly who the bogeyman is, we can't really name him or define him. In fact, in deference to gender-inclusive language, we should consider the possibility that the bogeyman is actually a bogeywoman! In any case, perhaps he (or she) represents all those things in the world that we don't yet know about but would be afraid of if we did.

As we grow older, feelings of fear remain with us, although the objects of our fear, or at least most of them, change. Teenagers may fear rejection or failure or being left out. Young adults may fear never being able to find a life partner or a fulfilling career. Many parents who thought they had overcome their fears find themselves living the fears of their children—they fear for their children's safety or perhaps an unwanted pregnancy. Older persons typically fear losing their independence, their health, their mobility, or their capacity to support themselves financially.

Surveys reveal that one of life's most common fears is the fear of getting up in front of an audience and giving a speech. And many people of all ages struggle with fears of the unknown, including the fear of death.

The Dr. Seuss story *What Was I Scared Of?* addresses the issue of fear. The story has just two characters: a cute-looking childlike "creacha" (a Seuss-style child) and an un-embodied pair of green pants. The cute little thing encounters the scary-looking pants on a dark path in the night. The "creacha" turns in the other direction and runs away as fast as he can. He tells himself he's not afraid of the pants, but it doesn't work. Every time he sees them, he is filled with fear. He turns and runs away.

The little guy's fear of the green pants is clearly having a negative impact on his life. He no longer goes to places he used to go. He doesn't do some of the things he likes to do, because he doesn't want to risk meeting up with the green pants. He can no longer go to Grin-itch to fetch Grin-itch spinach. He can't go fishing, because "green pants" knows how to row a boat.

Many of us can identify with the little guy. Our fears are preventing us from accomplishing our full potential. Perhaps there are places we would like to go, people we would like to get to know. Maybe we sense that God is calling us to a particular kind of service or ministry. But our fears are holding us back. Maybe it's fear that life could get too complicated or too busy. Perhaps it's the fear of the unknown. Like the little creacha, we realize that there is more to life, but fear stands in the way of pursuing it.

Theologically speaking, the opposite of fear is faith. The presence of faith does not automatically remove fears. Rather, faith provides us with the discipline, confidence, and courage to move forward in spite of our fears. Our faith reaffirms for us that God is ultimately in control of our lives. It has been said that there is no safer place to be than at the center of God's will. Thus, if we are confident that we are pursuing the will of God, we can also believe that our fears, though real, ought not paralyze us, ought not keep us from doing what is right.

It's hard to imagine anyone being more afraid than Jesus must have been in the garden of Gethsemane. Exactly when Jesus realized what his ultimate mission on earth would be is a question for theologians to debate. But it is clear from his agony in the garden that he knew at that point what was coming. He knew that the path before him would include a horrifying and painful death. Not only would it be physically painful, but it would be humiliating. He was soon to feel abandoned—fully and completely—by the Father he had served so well.

And he was afraid. "If it is possible, let this cup pass from me," he prayed. But he did not allow this unspeakable fear to keep him from pressing on to accomplish his earthly mission. He did not run away from his fears. He faced them head on.

Dr. Seuss also helps us to understand the secret to overcoming our fears. The secret is not to run faster or farther in the opposite direction. That only enables us to avoid our fears for a little while longer, but not to overcome them. The only way to overcome our fears is to face them. We've all heard the advice that the best way to get rid of an enemy is to make that enemy a friend. The same can be said of our fears. The best way to get rid of our fears is to make them our friends.

That is what the little creacha in the story did, although it was not by choice that he ended up face to face with the green pants. He started yelling and screaming, shrieking and howling. Was this the end?

> "But then a strange thing happened.
> Why, those pants began to cry!
> Those pants began to tremble.
> They were just as scared as I!"

The next thing you know, the little creacha has a new friend: a green one with two legs. In the facing of his fear he was able to discover that it was not as bad as he'd thought. In fact, it didn't need to be feared at all.

We need to hear it again: we cannot overcome fears by running from them. Someone who, as a child, was bitten by a dog may, quite understandably, have a fear of dogs into adulthood. If this person wants to overcome that fear, however, the way to do so is not by avoiding canines but by reaching out to them—literally, in this case.

What might happen in our Christian lives if we, too, faced our fears instead of running from them? Might it free us to do things that we've always wanted to do but were afraid to try? Or perhaps something that we once enjoyed doing but are afraid to try again?

I'm always amazed to hear about someone being afraid of something that he or she has never even tried. Some people who are afraid of flying have never been to an airport, let alone set foot on a plane. Some people are afraid of big cities even though they've never been to one. Some people are afraid of those from another ethnic group even though they've never met a person of the feared ethnicity.

Our fears may well be keeping us from effective Christian ministry. Someone is afraid of reaching out to the new neighbor in need: "I'm already busy enough, and I'm afraid that if I help, it will take up more time than I have to give." Someone else has always had a heart for the poor but is afraid to volunteer to take meals to the homeless because the shelter is located in an unsafe part of town.

Another person has always wanted to donate blood, but she's afraid of the pinch of the needle, even though others have told her that it really doesn't hurt that much. Still another person has long thought about being a missionary overseas, or at least going on a short-term mission project, but he's afraid of coming back with some rare, incurable disease, even though others from his church have made the trip safely.

Fears limit our ability to reach our potential as individual human beings and as the church, the bride of Christ. We must recognize that the kingdom of God is not a passive institution but a proactive one. Christ did not call us to sit in our living rooms and watch TV, to be content only with having our personal affairs under control. Rather, Christ calls us to go out into the world to make disciples, to bring justice to our communities, and to look after the hungry, the widow, the orphan, and the prisoner. We cannot fulfill this calling if we are paralyzed into inactivity by a fear of getting hurt, or making mistakes, or getting involved in messy or complicated situations. That is the path of fear, not the path of faith.

Think about what your fears are. What is holding you back?

What is keeping you from being all you can be and all you would like to be? Once you've identified them, face them. Talk about them. Seek advice. Find others who have had the same or similar fears and have overcome them, people who have found that moving forward in faith resulted in the realization that fear is often more imagined than real.

The little creacha, as a result of facing his fears, not only got his old life back but he also gained a new friend. Don't keep running. Faith will win out over fear every time.

CHAPTER 4

The Cat in the Hat Comes Back

When you stretch out your hands,
   I will hide my eyes from you;
even though you make many prayers,
   I will not listen;
   your hands are full of blood.
Wash yourselves:; make yourselves clean;
   remove the evil of your doings
   from before my eyes;
cease to do evil,
   learn to do good;
seek justice,
   rescue the oppressed,
defend the orphan,
   plead for the widow.
Come now, let us argue it out,
   says the LORD:
though your sins are like scarlet,
   they shall be like snow;
though they are red like crimson,
   they shall become like wool.
If you are willing and obedient,
   you shall eat the good of the land;

but if you refuse and rebel,
   you shall be devoured by the sword;
      for the mouth of the LORD has spoken.
(Isaiah 1:15-20)

This was no time for play.
This was no time for fun.
This was no time for games.
There was work to be done.
All that deep,
Deep, deep snow,
All that snow had to go....
We were working like that.
And then who should come up
But the CAT IN THE HAT!

As with some other Dr. Seuss characters, the Cat in the Hat is hard to pin down, hard to figure. He makes a very good first impression—seems innocent enough. But clearly he has a penchant for making messes, for getting himself into trouble and, more importantly, getting others into trouble. Is he ultimately a force for good? Or is he a force for not-so-good? It's hard to consider him "evil," because he seems only to want to have a fun time. On the other hand, he seems to press on with his plan without regard for what other people think or feel. Yet ultimately, he always saves the day by cleaning up whatever mess he has created.

We probably all have people in our lives, maybe even some friends or family members, who remind us of the Cat in the Hat. People we don't like but can't hate. People who make us nervous because they won't consider, let alone heed, sound advice. People who always seem to come out of any situation smelling like the proverbial rose, leaving nothing behind except the stress created by whatever mess they made. People who are too good to put in jail, but bad enough that you don't want to be walking the streets with them.

We also can identify with the messy situations that the mischievous Cat in the Hat creates. In *The Cat in the Hat Comes Back*, the Cat invites himself into the house of a couple of small children whose parents are not home. He decides to take a bath, and he ends up leaving behind a horrendous-looking pink bathtub ring. The ring comes off the tub okay—right onto the mother's new white dress, and then onto the wall, the rug, and so on. They finally at least get it out of the house. But then there are pink spots all over the snow.

The Cat needs help. And he gets it from twenty-six other, smaller cats (Cats A through Z), who seem only to make the problem worse or, at best, merely transfer it from one place to another. The pink snow situation seems hopeless to the two little children, who no doubt wish that the Cat in the Hat simply would have minded his own business that day.

Most of us can identify with the pink snow situation, because we have our own messes with which to contend. Well-intentioned people create problems. And sometimes we are the well-intentioned people who are creating the problems. We ask for help, but sometimes the helpers seem only to make things worse.

Our faith, in particular the theology of the fall, includes the affirmation that the world is a messy place:

> In the beginning when God created the heavens and the earth.... So God created humankind in his image, in the image of God created them; male and female he created them. God blessed them, and God said to them, "Be fruitful and

23

multiply, and fill the earth and subdue it...."
God saw everything that he had made, and
indeed, it was very good. (Genesis 1:1,27-
28,31)

The whole creation—birds and bees, flowers and trees, and
people—was, in the beginning, very good. But as folks went
about life in this good creation, trash began to appear: an apple
core, a torn fig leaf, a slain brother. Fast-forward to the twenty-
first century, and we have all kinds of messes. Pink snow looks
good compared to polluted rivers and skies and hazardous-waste
sites. Like children on Christmas morning, human beings have,
to a large degree, grabbed the gifts of creation and left piles and
piles of trash behind.

But the messes of our world are not just physical messes. We
have collectively created messes of a far more painful sort.
Around the world, those in power have placed pride ahead of
people, resulting in a mass of organized violence with no end in
sight. In our homes, children and spouses are being abused.
Homeless persons wander our streets like discarded fast-food
bags. All this goes on despite Jesus' teaching that when we tram-
ple on or ignore the "least of these," we are doing so to him too.

In fact, Jesus sternly warns those who would call a brother or
sister a fool. It's like killing them, he says, for those who do so
have failed to recognize in others the gift of life. Dire consequences await those who regard other people merely as things to
be used for selfish ends.

History is rife with accounts of humankind's inhumanity.
Through the ages, we have "trashed" God's world and God's
people. Much of this trashing we direct toward ourselves.
Despite efforts to raise awareness about the dangers of drugs, our
young people, and some who are not so young, still engage in

self-destructive behavior, behavior that belies the fact that life is a gift and that each person is to be treasured.

Many of our young people have learned such behavior from adults who don't value themselves, who abuse both illegal and legal drugs, alcohol, and tranquilizers. More and more people of all ages, especially youth it seems, after making messes in their lives that they feel cannot be cleaned up, decide to trash themselves by taking a gun to their head or by overdosing on drugs. Others do not take their lives, but respond less dramatically by withdrawing into a world of isolation and defeat. They resign from true living, choosing instead merely to exist. Having given up on all their hopes and dreams, they just hang on until life ends. For some, the messes that we have created or inherited overwhelm all hope of ever being cleaned up.

The good news is that it doesn't have to be this way. Isaiah spoke to a people surrounded by destruction in a world crumbling from without and within. He spoke words of hope that no matter how scarlet, how severe their sin appeared, God could take it away, and they could start over again. Or, they could reject the new path, and thus be destroyed.

The Cat in the Hat Comes Back has a happy ending. The smallest cat of the whole bunch (Cat Z) finally brings the solution to the problem. He has the power to clean up the mess once and for all. Cat Z has what Dr. Seuss calls a "Voom." This Voom, though small, has the power to put the whole house in order—to clean up the snow and restore everything to the way it is meant to be.

For Christians, this Voom is the restoring power that came in Jesus Christ. Jesus brings glad tidings of great joy. He is our Savior, our God, who came into the world we trashed to collect all the garbage, all the sin that clutters our world and makes our lives so full of messes. Christ soaked up the tears, the blood we have spilled. And carrying these, he climbed to a dumping ground for humans who were considered to have no worth. On a cross, on a hill called Calvary, he disposed of the trash, all the sins of the world.

Hear the good news: Even though human beings tried to dispose of Jesus, and evil hearts sought to bury him away, never to be heard from again, God raised him from the dead and gave him the power of everlasting life.

We find in the book of Revelation a vision of a new order, of a redeemed creation:

> Then I saw a new heaven and a new earth; for the first heaven and the first earth had passed away, and the sea was no more. And I saw the holy city, the new Jerusalem, coming down out of heaven from God, prepared as a bride adorned for her husband. And I heard a loud voice from the throne saying,
>
> "See, the home of God is among mortals.
> He will dwell with them as their God;
> they will be his peoples,
> and God himself will be with them;
> he will wipe every tear from their eyes.
> Death will be no more;
> mourning and crying and pain will be no more,
> for the first things have passed away."
>
> And the one who was seated on the throne said, "See, I am making all things new." Also he said, "Write this, for these words are trustworthy and true." (Revelation 21:1-5)

No matter where our messes came from or how unconquerable they seem, we worship a God for whom no mess is too messy. For all who trust in God, life can begin again today. God can take your sin and mine and erase it today. God can take our brokenness and make us whole. All can begin life anew in Jesus Christ. The apostle Paul knew about this fresh start in Jesus Christ: "So if anyone is in Christ, there is a new creation: everything old has passed away; see, everything has become new!" (2 Corinthians 5:17).

In small towns and suburbs across the nation, people put out their garbage on the curb if they want it hauled away. Christ invites us to do this very thing with the garbage that has found its way into our lives. We can place it on the curb, knowing that the Lord will soon pass by to take it away so that we can be reshaped to become the persons God intends us to be.

CHAPTER 5

The Zax

A few days later the younger son gathered all he had and traveled to a distant country, and there he squandered his property in dissolute living. When he had spent everything, a severe famine took place throughout that country, and he began to be in need. So he went and hired himself out to one of the citizens of that country, who sent him to his fields to feed the pigs. He would gladly have filled himself with the pods that the pigs were eating; and no one gave him anything. But when he came to himself he said, 'How many of my father's hired hands have bread enough and to spare, but here I am dying of hunger! I will get up and go to my father, and I will say to him, "Father, I have sinned against heaven and before you; I am no longer worthy to be called your son; treat me like one of your hired hands."(Luke 15:13-19)

Conventional wisdom holds that pride is the deadliest of the seven deadly sins. And the deadly power of pride is aptly illustrated both by the Dr. Seuss story *The Zax* and by the well-known Gospel story of the prodigal son.

In Dr. Seuss's imaginative world there are two kinds of Zaxes: those who go north and those who go south. As youngsters, the North-Going Zaxes learned in North-Going School to go north, exclusively. The South-Going Zaxes, quite naturally, learned to go south. The truth is that both kinds of Zaxes are capable of going in either direction—or east or west, for that matter. So their training, it seems, was focused not so much on what they are *able* to do, but rather on what they should *choose* to do.

One day, the inevitable comes to pass. A North-Going Zax finds himself on a collision course with a South-Going Zax. The two are moving in exactly opposite directions. And neither will budge. Now it would be one thing if these two Zaxes had come head to head on a narrow path or a one-lane bridge. Then some friction between them would be understandable. But instead, they arrive at their impasse in the middle of a desert expanse that seems to go on forever in all directions. Either Zax could take a single step right or left. Or, both Zaxes could agree to take half a sideways step in opposite directions so that each, after an ever-so-subtle detour, could resume moving in his chosen direction. But no. That won't do. Because the issue here has nothing to do with what is possible, with what *could be done* to solve the problem. Rather, for both Zaxes, this is a matter of pride.

> "*Never budge!* That's my rule. *Never budge in the least!*
> *Not an inch to the west! Not an inch to the east!*
> I'll stay here, not budging! I can and I will
> If it makes you and me and the whole world stand still!"

When one Zax tells the other that he won't budge for fifty-nine days if that's what it takes to win this little skirmish, the other responds by upping the ante to fifty-nine years! (Apparently, the Zax species never has to eat or use the restroom.)

Both Zaxes come across as being foolish—prime targets for head-shaking laughter and ridicule. But before we laugh too hard, we may want to consider the Zaxes we've encountered in our own lives, including in the church. And it may be an even better idea for us to search for the Zax within ourselves. We will always have trouble growing as individuals and as the community of Christ if we are unwilling to change, unwilling to budge, unwilling to consider someone else's feelings and perspectives.

The fundamental flaw in both the North-Going Zax and the South-Going Zax is pride. If we are honest, we will acknowledge that this same fundamental problem permeates human relationships in many different settings: internationally, nationally, and domestically in our communities and our families.

Sometimes it's hard to read the daily newspaper because it teems with accounts of violence around the world—people fighting people for reasons that, more often than not, are not altogether clear. Sometimes the combatants are still in their youth—children young enough to be playing with toys, but instead wielding deadly weapons.

Typically, they are fighting wars that began decades, or even centuries, ago. These young people cannot possibly know what they are fighting for, but they learned in their own version of Zax school to go in only one direction and to recognize only one way to understand and interpret their world. People on all sides of various conflicts who cannot see the Zax in themselves have put pride and ideology ahead of innocent people, ahead of life itself. Either side is capable of budging, but neither side will—not for fifty-nine years or, perhaps, even fifty-nine thousand years.

In our own society we see Zaxes dominating our political system—ideologues of one brand or another who are unwilling even to listen to other perspectives, let alone to consider compromising. Our leaders rarely admit that they may have been wrong about something. Thus, they are unable to change or grow, because to change suggests that something was wrong before, and the pride of the Zax would never allow that.

Each time I read about a labor strike, whether by baseball players or schoolteachers or electricians, I am reminded of Zaxes. The sad truth is that if neither Zax is willing to budge, then both Zaxes ultimately lose. They spend a lifetime never budging. When workers go on strike, it seems that the common sense thing to do is for both sides to agree to the recommendations of a wise and neutral third party, someone capable of seeing all perspectives and of providing a direction that can move everyone off the common path to destruction. But such an approach cannot work because it is too rational. And pride does not understand the word "rational." Pride would rather self-destruct than change.

This is not to say that we should never uphold and cling to our principles. In fact, there is something highly admirable in those who stand up for their moral principles regardless of the cost for doing so. But a personal preference or prejudice is something very different from a moral principle. We must distinguish between boldly standing to uphold clear biblical principles and stubbornly clinging to beliefs and ideas that have no clear basis in Scripture but instead have wrongly been raised to the level of moral absolutes.

The problem of pride hits us not just on international and national levels. Its insidious poison also attacks our families. Parents and children are estranged. A brother and sister haven't talked for years. Husbands and wives hold grudges.

31

Sometimes no one can remember what exactly led to the estrangement in the first place. But both sides are "dug in," too proud to admit any wrongdoing and to reach out to heal the wounds.

The story of the prodigal son illustrates the power of pride at various points. We have no reason to think that the father in the story has been anything but a good father to his two sons. But his younger son wants his inheritance early, which is his way of saying that as far as he's concerned, his father is dead. The boy wants his independence. His pride has convinced him that he doesn't need anyone, including his family, to find his way in this world. He can make it on his own.

The world, however, offers up a heavy dose of reality. He finds, as many young people have found through the years, that life on the outside is not as breezy as they thought it would be. All of a sudden, mom's cooking doesn't seem all that bad. In fact, it seems downright delicious.

One wonders how may times the prodigal son thought about going home before having to go all the way to the bottom to recover his senses. But his Zax-like pride stopped him. For going home meant having to admit that he was wrong. And he couldn't do that. Not unless he had no other choice.

That's exactly what it means to hit bottom: to have no other choice. The grip of pride, along with the denial that accompanies it, is so strong that as long as people have just a hint of a choice, they will not give in. Which is why we nod our heads to the conventional wisdom that a person has to hit bottom before he or she can turn things around. Only the absolute bottom— when there is nowhere else to go, no other choice to make—can break the grip of pride and set a person on a different path.

With no lower place to go than living among pigs, the prodigal son returns. He doesn't have to say he's sorry or admit being wrong. His act of returning does that for him. The very fact that he's home means that he's swallowed his pride.

Then we encounter the father's grace. He doesn't punish his son or put him to work. More importantly, he doesn't communicate "I told you so" either by his words or by his actions. Instead, he throws a party.

Now the pride of the older brother kicks in. In fact, he is a prodigal in his own way. One can only wonder how this blow to his pride—his father throwing a party for his younger brother—affected the family dynamics for years to come.

The older brother's pride was prompting him to say, "I told you so. You were wrong." Breaking the grip of pride, however, entails not worrying about who was right or wrong. Putting the past behind and embracing the freshness of a brand new start overpower any compulsions to keep score. And if we don't keep score, everyone can be a winner.

The story of the Zax, unlike most Dr. Seuss stories, has an unhappy ending. A whole world gets built around the North-Going and the South-Going Zaxes—a world with cars and buildings and bridges. The longer they have stood there, the less room they now have to move in a direction. Their pride has hardened, and an end to their impasse is nowhere in sight.

We know from our faith that God is not a God who keeps score. Like the shepherd in search of the lost sheep, God is not concerned about how we got lost. He's just happy to have us home. We never need to allow pride to stand in the way of returning to God, who will always run out into the field to meet us and welcome us with open arms.

In the midst of strained relationships with others—parents, children, brothers, sisters—perhaps the same can be true. Will we allow pride to stand in the way, or are we willing to take the risk that comes with reaching out? This is a risk that admits we may have been wrong, that opens the door for others to say, "I told you so." But remember, that other person might say, "I was wrong, too."

There is never a better time than now to take a risk to heal a broken relationship—especially when the only other option is to stand in the desert for fifty-nine years nose to nose with a Zax.

CHAPTER 6

How the Grinch Stole Christmas!

He entered Jericho and was passing through it. A man was there named Zacchaeus; he was a chief tax collector and was rich. He was trying to see who Jesus was, but on account of the crowd he could not, because he was short in stature. So he ran ahead and climbed a sycamore tree to see him, because he was going to pass that way. When Jesus came to the place, he looked up and said to him, "Zacchaeus, hurry and come down; for I must stay at your house today." So he hurried down and was happy to welcome him. (Luke 19:1-6)

Arguably, the most widely known character created by Dr. Seuss is the inimitable Grinch. This most unusual character, who is at once both lovable and "hateable," is immortalized in the book *How the Grinch Stole Christmas!* and also by the animated television special of the same name. For millions of children (and adults) over the past several decades, Christmas just isn't Christmas without at least one viewing of this classic work of art. More recently, Hollywood further ingrained the character of the Grinch into the public's consciousness through a movie starring the talented comic actor Jim Carrey as the Grinch.

The story of the Grinch reinforces the Gospel message on several different levels and in more than one way. Of course, it is not the Grinch, but the *Whos* down in *Who*-ville who provide the most fundamental lesson of this story. This lesson from the *Whos* is the subject of chapter 12, but in this chapter we focus on three lessons we can learn not from the *Whos*, but from the Grinch, who, if we look closely at him, can teach us something about others and, more importantly, about ourselves.

The Grinch is an altogether miserable fellow. Whereas some would look at a glass of water and call it half empty while others would say it's half full, the Grinch likely would say that it doesn't matter whether the glass is half empty or half full because the water probably is contaminated anyway. In other words, the Grinch goes well beyond mere pessimism; the Grinch is a totally negative person.

Our natural reaction when we encounter such angry, despicable, miserable people is to wonder why. Who did something to this person to provoke such anger? What happened to cause such a negative approach to life? In the case of the Grinch, no one seems to know:

> It *could* be his head wasn't screwed on just right.
> It *could* be, perhaps, that his shoes were too tight.
> But I think that the most likely reason of all
> May have been that his heart was two sizes too small.

If we could isolate one thing in the story that makes the Grinch most angry, most miserable, it is this: other people's happiness. The Grinch seems somewhat content in his own misery until he witnesses others who don't share in his misery, others—namely, the *Whos*—who have found happiness, contentment, love.

We've all heard the quip "Misery loves company." Well, the Grinch's problem is that he is miserable—extremely, intolerably miserable—but he has no one to keep him company in his misery. So, having no company, he sets out to create some. The Grinch reasons that if he can't be happy, he'll fix things so that no one can be happy. And he targets those despicable *Whos*.

The Grinch's whole motivation for trying to ruin, to "steal" Christmas, is to drag other people down to his level of misery and discontent. The Grinch is captive to one of the seven deadly sins: envy. He is jealous. Because he is not happy, he can't stand other people being happy either.

In contrast, the clear message of Scripture is that we are to uplift other people—to rejoice in others' happiness, to assist others in their needs, and to support others in their sorrow. But if we are to learn from the Grinch, we must sincerely ask ourselves whether there are times and situations in our lives when we follow the example of the Grinch instead of following the message of Scripture.

We live in a highly competitive society, one that produces winners and losers, not only in sports, but also in the business world, in office settings, and even in the church. Are there times when we seek victory or some sense of solace by secretly rejoicing in others' misfortunes or failures? Are there times when we, like the Grinch, seek to raise ourselves up by dragging other people down with us?

As much as we must guard against this attitude in ourselves, we must also protect ourselves from the consequences of such attitudes when they emanate from others. I know of a girl who was a substitute on her junior high basketball team until the coach noticed how hard she played and how much she hustled. Finally, she got a chance to start a game, and for two or three games she made the most of it. But then some of the others on the team started talking, implying that the girl got to start because she was the "coach's pet." More concerned about peer relationships than about being a starter, the girl quit trying, quit hustling as much as before. And soon she was back on the bench. She had been dragged down to someone else's level.

Mature Christians are in tune with their feelings and in touch with their motives. They are open to changing when these feelings and motives are impure, but they are also firm in not allowing others to influence them when their motives are pure. Lesson one from the Grinch: we can't pull ourselves up by dragging other people down—and we shouldn't allow others to do so.

Lesson two focuses on how the Grinch became so "grinchy." Many Dr. Seuss purists were disappointed with the Hollywood version of the story, perhaps because it took some liberties with the original, but mostly because it could never be the same; a classic cannot be replaced. Nevertheless, one thing that the movie version did was enable viewers to consider how the Grinch got to be that way.

We see the Grinch as a child. He is very unpopular—an outcast. The other children ridicule him. It is in response to his pain and poor self-image that he flees to Mt. Crumpit to escape his tormentors and to wallow in his misery.

As Christians trying to minister to others in a hurting world, we will encounter people who are, for all intents and purposes, Grinches—angry, mean-spirited, and selfish. Being kind and polite to such "hard-to-love" persons is a challenge, to say the least. But, ironically, it is those people who need love the most who are the hardest to love.

If the goal is to learn to love a hard-to-love person, it helps to learn a little bit about how he or she got to be that way. One of the hardest-to-love people from the Gospel accounts is Zacchaeus. It seems that he managed to make an enemy of just about everyone. Sometimes I wonder whether people didn't like Zacchaeus because he was mean-spirited, or whether he was mean-spirited because people didn't like him. Perhaps it was a little, or a lot, of both. We know little about Zacchaeus's background. But we do know something important about him: he was short. And he must have been unusually short, or else the Gospel writer would not have made a point of it.

Perhaps Zacchaeus, like the Grinch, was a target of ridicule and scorn ever since he was a child. Perhaps he learned to hate and mistreat other people as a response to the pain that others had inflicted on him. If we think about it, probably all of us can identify a few Zacchaeuses we have known in our lives—people who have been hurt, people who need to be loved.

Zacchaeus needed someone to love him. And Jesus was the one who did just that. Instead of making him a target of ridicule, Jesus showed him respect, treated him not just as a human being—which would have been good enough for Zacchaeus—but as a special person. He went to be a guest in Zacchaeus's house. This not only made Zacchaeus's day; it changed his entire life. This expression of love and respect was enough to overcome all the pain that Zacchaeus had endured up to that point. He was a new person. He went from feeling unloved to learning to love, from hurting other people to helping other people.

If we are to follow Jesus, we too must learn to recognize and to love people who, like the Grinch, are miserable and difficult to love because they are in so much pain. Engulfed in their pain, they find it hard to think about anyone but themselves. If we can show such hard-to-love persons how it feels to be loved, perhaps they, like Zacchaeus, will be transformed.

Lesson three from the Grinch is closely related to the second. It is the message that people *can* change. This sounds at first like a simplistic message, but it is in fact a profound, even radical statement.

For many years, our culture has carried on a "nature versus nurture" debate. In essence, the debate centers on whether we became who we are because of our genetic makeup or because of our environment. What this debate overlooks is that nature and nurture are not the only factors. Biblical faith presupposes that regardless of our genetic makeup or the environments that shape us, we can make choices between right and wrong. People who have all the right genes and were brought up in an ideal, nurturing environment still can make bad choices, while those who seem to have both nature and nurture stacked against them can overcome them by making good choices. Human beings are more than the product of genes and environments. Christian theology rejects fatalism: God gave human beings free will with which to influence the reality that they experience.

The Grinch is a model of someone who, in a moment of realization, changed. It had nothing to do with nature or nurture. It had everything to do with a realization in his soul, with a change of heart.

> "And what happened *then*...?
> Well...in *Who*-ville they say
> That the Grinch's small heart
> Grew three sizes that day!

The change took place not as a result of force or torture or punishment for the Grinch's crime of stealing Christmas. Coercion can successfully modify a person's behavior, but it cannot change a person's heart. Change that rises up from within is inspired by a new insight, a new model, a new way of looking at things, a new set of priorities. This is what the unassuming *Whos* provided for the Grinch, perhaps without even realizing it. The Grinch's actions deserved punishment. But instead of punishment, those humble *Whos* gave the Grinch a healthy dose of grace. And it was enough to change him forever.

Let us never be held captive to the idea that people cannot change. In the end, even the Grinch knew better.

CHAPTER 7

Horton Hears a Who!

The earth is the LORD's and all that is in it,
the world, and those who live in it;
for he has founded it on the seas,
and established it on the rivers. (Psalm 24:1-2)

I consider that the sufferings of this present
time are not worth comparing with the glory
about to be revealed to us. For the creation
waits with eager longing for the revealing of the
children of God; for the creation was subjected
to futility, not of its own will but by the will of
the one who subjected it, in hope that the creation itself will be set free from its bondage to
decay and will obtain the freedom of the glory
of the children of God. We know that the
whole creation has been groaning in labor
pains until now; and not only the creation, but
we ourselves, who have the first fruits of the
Spirit, groan inwardly while we wait for adop-
tion, the redemption of our bodies. For in hope
we were saved. Now hope that is seen is not
hope. For who hopes for what is seen? But if

we hope for what we do not see, we wait for it
with patience. (Romans 8:18-25)

On the fifteenth of May, in the Jungle of Nool,
In the heat of the day, in the cool of the pool,
He was splashing...enjoying the jungle's
    great joys...
When Horton the elephant heard a small noise.
So Horton stopped splashing. He looked
    toward the sound,
"That's funny," thought Horton. "There is no
    one around."
Then he heard it again! Just a very faint yelp,
As if some tiny person were calling for help.
"I'll help you," said Horton. "But who are you?
    Where?"

Horton Hears a Who! is another Dr. Seuss story featuring that
large, loving, and lovable elephant Horton. In this story,
Horton, who always seems to function as a sort of God figure,
hears a sound that none of the other animals can hear. Their ears
are not sensitive enough to hear the cries of the Whos in Who-
ville. The Whos' entire world—replete with Whos of all ages,
with houses, and streets, and churches, and grocery stores—
exists on a tiny speck of dust too small for the elephant even to
see. But Horton can hear them loud and clear, and he makes it
his mission to protect his tiny friends. After all, Horton says that
a person is a person, no matter how small.

Horton carefully places the speck of dust that houses the
Whos' entire world onto a clover for safekeeping. The other animals, however, are convinced that Horton is off his rocker. They
decide not only to make fun of Horton, but also to take the

clover away. An eagle carries off the clover and ultimately drops it into a field with millions of other clovers, leaving Horton to search for the only one that houses the *Whos*. Thirteen million clovers later, Horton finally finds the one he is looking for. The *Whos* are a bit out of sorts, but they're okay.

By now, the other animals have grown tired of Horton's antics. They set out to put Horton in a cage and to boil the tiny speck of dust in a kettle of Beezle-Nut oil. Horton is desperate. He pleads with the *Whos* to make the loudest noise they can so that everyone can hear them and believe Horton. The *Whos* try, but it's not enough. Only Horton's ears are sensitive enough to hear. But finally, the mayor of *Who*-ville discovers that there is one small Who, in fact the smallest one of all, who was not making a sound. When this one joins the chorus, the rest of the animals are able to hear, and the town of *Who*-ville is saved.

In reading this story, we may find it easy to identify with the *Whos*. So much of the world is desperately trying to make a sound, but sometimes it seems that no one is listening or hearing. Indeed, in Romans we read about how all of creation is groaning and moaning for redemption. The Bible's most important message is that God came into this world through Jesus Christ in order to redeem humankind and, indeed, all creation. We can live with the confidence that although on earth our cries fall on many a deaf ear, the God who knows even the tiniest sparrow hears, Horton-like, the cries of the world.

At other times we may identify more with Horton in our efforts to hear the cries of a groaning world and come to its aid. Sometimes we have to work at interpreting and understanding the world's cries. Those of us who have pets have come to distinguish between particular kinds of barks or meows or whines. Many a mother can sleep through a myriad of noises during the night—rumbling traffic, a whirring air conditioner, howling wind or splashing rain—only to be instantly awakened by the faintest sound from her newborn child.

Humanity is unique in God's creation, but the Bible tells us that all creation is important to God, and human beings are to be faithful stewards of that creation. When I consider the passage from Romans about the whole creation groaning, I am reminded of that very difficult theological question, posed always, it seems, by a nine-year-old child, that all pastors at some point must answer: "Will my dog go to heaven?" (Or it might be a cat or a goldfish.)

When faced with a theological question that I can't figure out, I do what all preachers do: I quote somebody else. Here is how pastor Kel Groseclose wades through this quagmire:

> Having built such deep and lasting bonds it's natural for children to ask what happens when pets die. Do they go to heaven? Or as one girl inquired, "Do they have their very own heaven?" Another child experienced the loss of both her grandfather and her favorite pet within days of each other. She expressed her wonder in concrete terms. "Did Pasha go to heaven with Grandpa?" The best response to questions such as this that have no definite answers is to honestly share one's own feeling: "I loved Pasha just as you did and if the decision were mine, she would be curled up at Grandpa's feet right now." Jesus told the disciples, "About that day or hour no one knows" (Mark 13:32). We do not have sufficient information to make official pronouncements concerning eternity.

Yet, there's no harm in speculating, as long as we remain humble and draw from what we already know about God's nature. Personally I think heaven would be rather bland and boring if life in all its varieties weren't present. Every earthly expression of life is sacred to the Creator. We know that not even a tiny sparrow falls from the sky without God's awareness. God's love reaches out to the lost sheep. God picks up and holds the little lambs. It seems logical and fair that cats and dogs, goldfish and horses should have a place somewhere in everlasting life. God, who yearns for us to be caring and kind to all living creatures, also feels compassion for them. The God who makes baby animals so appealing and pets so loyal and faithful, surely has a warm spot for each and every one.[1]

I like this response because it reaffirms something that we so often forget: the earth is the Lord's and everything in it. God's compassion extends to all of creation, and human beings, as God's stewards, bear an obligation to respond to creation's cries.

For those who would like to consider this topic on a more sophisticated level than Dr. Seuss's writings or a pastor's musings with a nine-year-old child, there is Pierre Teilhard de Chardin, a scientist and Roman Catholic priest in the first part of the twentieth century. He was a paleontologist—someone who studies fossil remains. But in his role as a priest, one day in the Gobi Desert on an excavation he found that when time came to

---

1. Kel Groseclose, *Why Did God Make Bugs and Other Icky Things? Questions Kids Ask* (Nashville: Dimensions for Living, 1992), 17–18.

celebrate the Mass, he had no bread or wine, elements essential for this rite. This priest looked at the world around him, and the realization came to him on that day that although he had no bread or wine, all creation possessed a certain sacredness or holiness because of the essential mystery of the Christian faith proclaimed in John's Gospel: "The Word became flesh." In other words, God not only created this universe in which we live, replete with grandeur, but God also entered into it in Jesus Christ. God offered up the whole of creation as his gift, a sacrifice of praise and thanksgiving. God has entered into creation by Jesus coming and being present with us, thus leaving an eternal, indelible stamp on this world.

Let me encourage you to care for this world. We must not submit to greed, lust, and other forces that tend to destroy the wholeness of the creation of God in this world. The bottom line for us remains, as stated in Psalm 24, "The earth is the LORD's and all that is in it." We do not own the world. But as God's stewards and as participants in God's plan of redemption, we must hear and respond to the world's cries.

This responsibility includes the obligation to care for the earth. I am reminded of a story about a boy who wanted to be an usher in a nearby movie theater. During the interview, the manager of the theater asked him an important question: "Son, what would you do if we had a crowded theater and a fire broke out?" The boy thought for a minute and then replied, "Well, you don't have to worry about me. You don't have to worry about me at all. If it's a crowded theater and a fire breaks out, I would get out safely." Obviously, that wasn't the answer the manager was looking for, but it reflects the spirit of many of our answers to such questions. We think instinctively only about ourselves; it doesn't matter what happens to anyone else as long as I get out safely. That's not the answer Horton would give, nor should it be an answer for faithful Christians.

Among our responsibilities is that of preserving and protecting our planet. For too long, care for our environment has lacked an appropriate position on the church's agenda. Usually, concerns for economic growth win out over concerns for protecting and preserving the environment. But if the earth is the Lord's, we have no right to trash it. In fact, we have a responsibility to hear its groans and to respond.

This might make life inconvenient for us at times. It might mean avoiding certain products or cutting back on some activities that have been part of our lives. As we make sacrifices intended to preserve and protect the environment, it might help us to recognize that such sacrifice provides a common bond with those who have gone before us. After all, in previous generations in our culture and in others, the concept of preservation was instinctive. One might say that many of our grandparents were great recyclers way before the word "recycle" ever came to be. My grandparents' unused upstairs room was always full of glass jars of many kinds. They might be Mason jars with screw-on lids and replaceable tops. Or perhaps mayonnaise jars. Grandmother never threw a jar away. She washed them and kept them in that room until the pear tree had pears or the cherry tree had cherries. Then she filled those jars. If she didn't have the right lids, she put paraffin on top of the jelly to keep from having to throw away a jar.

In fact, I doubt that either of my grandmothers ever threw anything away. I still have a wonderful quilt that one of them made out of scraps she had saved. And my grandfather would never think of hauling away the waste from the farm. They found something to do with even the waste from the animals. One of the first toys I was given was a farm set that included a tractor with a manure spreader. I learned that even waste from the animals was not thrown away. It was too useful.

The whole concept of the family farm is rooted in the idea that one day it will belong to our children or to someone else. So we can't just plunder it for all we want. Our culture has lost a lot as it has become more and more detached from the soil. It is not as easy for us to hear the cries of the earth as it once was.

Sometimes I am concerned about the message advanced when we sing in church, "This earth is not my home; I am moving on to a better place." Many of our hymns have this imagery. And though it is important to affirm our belief in immortality, we need not and should not do so at the expense of the earth, which is a gift from God to be treasured and passed on to future generations.

There are so many little things the church can do to display sensitivity for hearing the earth's cries. My church once put up a little cup rack so that heavy-duty coffee drinkers have mugs on hand. I was amazed at how it cut down on the need for paper cups. I had another group that washed dishes every time they ate. We all need to do more and more of this, not because we have to, but because it's right, because the earth is the Lord's and everything in it. We must hear its cries.

And we must, like Horton, hear the cries of other people, no matter how small or insignificant they may be in the world's eyes. If anything, Scripture instructs us to take special care of those people—especially widows, orphans, and prisoners—who are downtrodden and have been marginalized from the spheres of influence in our society.

This includes people who cannot afford to wear the clothes or drive the cars that are considered essential to being successful in our society. It means making more room for people from ethnic minority groups who are denied their rights to full humanity in both overt and subtle ways. It means that no child should ever be labeled a "dummy" or a "geek" or a "nerd." And certainly no child or spouse should ever be subjected to the trashing of physical or emotional abuse. All of these are among the *Whos* whose cries we need to listen for with greater sensitivity and respond to with a greater sense of urgency and concern.

The world belongs to God. Each of us is stamped with God's image. And God's world has been redeemed. Not only did God create this world and call it good, but also when God saw what a mess we had made of it, God came in Jesus Christ to renew and restore the world. Christ came and lived among us until people trashed and dumped him outside Jerusalem for being in the way. The good news for us this day is that Jesus didn't stay trashed. He lives again, and he provides his followers with redeeming power that allows them to hear the world's moans and groans as they wait for and work toward its full redemption.

Let us, like the *Whos*, remember that no matter how weak our cries may be, God is listening. Let us also, like Horton, always be listening for cries that others are not yet able to hear. And most importantly, let's step in and make a difference.

CHAPTER 8

Green Eggs and Ham

The hand of the LORD came upon me, and he brought me out by the spirit of the LORD and set me down in the middle of a valley; it was full of bones. He led me all around them; there were very many lying in the valley, and they were very dry. He said to me, "Mortal, can these bones live?" I answered, "O Lord GOD, you know." Then he said to me, "Prophesy to these bones, and say to them: O dry bones, hear the word of the LORD. Thus says the Lord GOD to these bones: I will cause breath to enter you, and you shall live. I will lay sinews on you, and will cause flesh to come upon you, and cover you with skin, and put breath in you, and you shall live; and you shall know that I am the LORD."

So I prophesied as I had been commanded; and as I prophesied, suddenly there was a noise, a rattling, and the bones came together, bone to its bone. I looked, and there were sinews on them, and flesh had come upon them, and skin had covered them; but there was not breath in them. Then he said to me, "Prophesy to the breath, prophesy, mortal, and say to the breath: Thus says the Lord GOD: Come from the four winds, O breath, and breathe upon these slain, that they may live." I prophesied as he commanded me, and the breath came into them, and they lived, and stood on their feet, a vast multitude.

Then he said to me, "Mortal, these bones are the whole house of Israel. They say, 'Our bones are dried up, and our hope is lost; we are cut off completely.'" (Ezekiel 37:1-11)

For the love of Christ urges us on, because we are convinced that one has died for all; therefore all have died. And he died for all, so that those who live might live no longer for themselves, but for him who died and was raised for them. From now on, therefore, we regard no one from a human point of view; even though we once knew Christ from a human point of view, we know him no longer in that way. So if anyone is in Christ, there is a new creation: everything old has passed away; see, everything has become new! All this is from God, who reconciled us to himself through Christ, and has given us the ministry of reconciliation; that is, in Christ God was reconciling the world to himself, not counting their trespasses against them, and entrusting the message of reconciliation to us. So we are ambassadors for Christ, since God is making his appeal through us; we entreat you on behalf of

Christ, be reconciled to God.
 (2 Corinthians 5:14-20)

Do you like green eggs and ham?
I do not like them, Sam-I-am.
I do not like green eggs and ham....
Would you like them in a house?
Would you like them with a mouse?...
Would you eat them in a box?
Would you eat them with a fox?...
Would you? Could you? In a car?
Eat them! Eat them! Here they are!

Dr. Seuss's well-known, playful, poetic story *Green Eggs and Ham* features an odd but persistent little character who calls himself "Sam-I-am." Sam's mission throughout the story is to persuade (compel, hound, badger) another character, whose name is never revealed, to sample a rather unusual dish: green eggs and ham. The target of Sam's pursuit, even though he has never tried them, insists throughout that he does not like green eggs and ham. It's hard to blame Sam's friend for being so sure of what he likes and doesn't like. After all, there are plenty of people who would never eat anything green, especially if it's something that isn't supposed to be green or wasn't originally green!

But in the end, Sam-I-am gets his wish. Worn weary from Sam's persistence, the other fellow finally tries green eggs and ham. And wonder of wonders, he likes them! He ends up thanking Sam for introducing him to a new dish.

So many times in life we, like Sam's friend, initially resist something that ultimately we might like, or something that ultimately we need whether we like it or not. We are hesitant to try new things, resistant to hearing new ideas or perspectives, especially when those new perspectives make us uncomfortable. Perhaps they require some serious self-inspection or urge us to get outside the comfort zones of things familiar.

The Old Testament prophet Ezekiel reminds me of Sam-I-am. He is handed a plate of green eggs and ham in the form of a scroll "with words of lamentation and mourning and woe" (Ezekiel 2:10). The scroll symbolizes the entrée—the message—that Ezekiel is to offer to the children of Israel. Ezekiel has sampled the entrée, and the message is "sweet as honey" as far as he is concerned. Yet it is not surprising that Ezekiel receives the warning that the children of Israel might not agree with his tastes in cuisine. In fact, they might refuse to hear what he has to say, opting instead to tell Ezekiel that he can keep his green eggs and ham—all his lamentation, mourning, and woe!

Yes, Ezekiel had an unappetizing, unpopular message for the people of Israel. But it was a necessary one. Hard times had come to Israel. It was around 587 B.C.E., and the nation had been destroyed. Now, this was a nation that believed it had been uniquely chosen by God and was somehow invincible because God was on its side. Yet Babylonian warriors, who did not even believe in the one true God, the mighty one of Israel, conquered this nation. These people in exile—refugees from their own, beloved homeland—certainly wanted a message from God. But they didn't want anything remotely resembling green eggs and ham. They wanted words of comfort, words of assurance, something to make them feel better in their time of despair. Many of Ezekiel's words did not suit their taste.

In fact, the message that Ezekiel received and was compelled to proclaim included words of judgment and warning of more destruction yet to come. It had become the habit of some folks around Ezekiel to hope and pray for a return to the "good old days." But part of Ezekiel's proclamation was that those good old days really weren't so good after all. Ezekiel observed that Israel had acted like an unfaithful mate, pursuing one center of power after another, forming alliances with anyone and anything, even when such activity compromised their devotion to the Lord.

The children of Israel were a rebellious people who, time after time, confused or ignored their priorities. Covenants with God were replaced by covenants with neighbor states. Devotion to God was replaced by devotion to self. And so Ezekiel proclaimed that the inhabitants of Jerusalem had become like the wood of a wild vine, fit for nothing but destruction, useful only as fuel for a fire. In large part, Ezekiel's message was hard to digest because he was not content to keep things vague or general. Instead of blaming the problems of the times on the nation as a whole, he brought the message close to home by focusing on individual responsibility. Each man, woman, and child of Israel was responsible.

Today, we certainly can relate to this dynamic. When there are problems, we are prone to blame such vague entities as the economy or the government, or big business or politicians. This relieves us of any personal responsibility. It relieves us of the responsibility to zero in on our own attitudes and behavior. We are far better at blaming the government than we are at accepting individual responsibility. We don't like to think about how the ways in which we spend money, or how our wasteful patterns of consumption, might negatively affect the environment or create situations of injustice for people in other parts of the world. It's far easier to insist that we don't like green eggs and ham than it is to try on a new way of looking at things, especially if the new message might reflect negatively on what we've been doing up to now.

Ezekiel, much to the dismay of those who shun green eggs and ham, devotes an entire chapter (Ezekiel 18) to the problem of individual guilt and responsibility. We read, "Therefore I will judge you, O house of Israel, all of you according to your ways, says the Lord GOD" (Ezekiel 18:30). Ezekiel could see that many of the problems that his people faced were magnified by the failure of individuals to assume responsibility. In exile, the Judean refugees neglected worship, failed to build proper houses for their families, and sat mourning their losses while the few remnants of their culture and the last vestiges of their faith continued to deteriorate.

In what ways are contemporary Americans like the Israelites of Bible times? How seriously do we, especially Christians, regard the individual responsibilities that we have toward neighbor, church, family, and our country? I've heard many a minister lament the fact that it is so hard these days to find people to teach Sunday school, work with youth, or serve on a church committee. And then we wonder why our churches are not growing, or why so many of our young people have strayed from the church.

Ezekiel's message to the children of Israel thousands of years ago is also a message for us today. We have every right to look after our own personal needs and desires. God wants us to enjoy life. But we must balance our desires for personal comfort and prosperity with responsibilities to other people and other institutions, especially if we want those institutions to endure and thrive. That means that often we must act not in the hope or expectation of an immediate personal reward, but rather for the long-term best interest of everyone, including ourselves. Therefore, sometimes in our lives, we may have to become

Ezekiel. That is, we may have to take a stand and deliver messages that will, perhaps even among our friends, be rejected like Sam's green eggs and ham.

As we are emboldened to take such stands, we can find encouragement in the rest of what Ezekiel has to say. His message is colored by the vision of a chariot borne aloft by winged cherubim and mounted upon wheels within wheels that could fly or roll in all directions. This extraordinary vision proclaimed that God was not confined to a temple or even to Israel itself. Rather, the vision proclaimed that God was present wherever his children roamed. In whatever sphere of life—work, school, or leisure—our obligations to our Lord continue. Our lives are lived in the Lord God's presence.

It is within the context of this theme of God's presence that Ezekiel's green eggs and ham became sweet. For just as we cannot get away from God, neither can we be cut off from the Lord. God's people are never forgotten. In strange lands and strange places, God is there. God is there also when we find ourselves in our own kinds of strange lands and places. For captives in Babylon, for people cut off from those they love, for folks who are separated from the things they prize most highly and hold most dear, the assurance of God's presence is the beginning of hope. We know what Ezekiel proclaimed: God is not only our judge, but also our redeemer and sustainer.

Ezekiel's message of judgment is also a message of grace and of hope. God's people are not forgotten. The Lord is the good shepherd who cares for his sheep. It is in the pages of Ezekiel that we read these words:

> For thus says the Lord GOD: I myself will search
> for my sheep, and will seek them out. As

> shepherds seek out their flocks when they are
> among their scattered sheep, so I will seek out
> my sheep. I will rescue them from all the places
> to which they have been scattered on a day of
> clouds and thick darkness.... They shall know
> that I, the LORD their God, am with them, and
> that they, the house of Israel, are my people, says
> the Lord GOD. You are my sheep, the sheep of
> my pasture, and I am your God, says the Lord
> GOD. (Ezekiel 34:11-12,30-31)

In another vision, Ezekiel views a field full of dead, dry bones. These bones, like the Jolly Roger flag or the poison warning logo, are symbols of death, destruction, and decay. But these dead, dry bones rattle and rise before Ezekiel's eyes. And Ezekiel knows that the Lord God Almighty can bring new life even where there appears to be no hope. Israel may feel cut off. The people may despair of any salvation. You or I may sink into the darkest pit and see it close around us, but like the dry bones of the valley, we can rise again through the renewing power of the Spirit of the living God. It is amazing how the realization of God's presence and a fuller appreciation of God's power and love can make green eggs and ham taste like milk and honey. God's renewing grace is all around us.

Let us proclaim Ezekiel's message. Whether or not it is well received, it is the message of Ezekiel that God is the judge of our nation, of all nations, and the judge of our lives and all lives. We all stand accountable, and God's presence reaches into every corner of our existence. We cannot ignore it; God's judgment is present. But with the judgment comes the forgiving grace calling us back like sheep gone astray, renewing our lives, breathing a new spirit into our dry bones. Heed these words from the book of Ezekiel:

> Therefore I will judge you, O house of Israel, all of you according to your ways, says the Lord GOD. Repent and turn from all your transgressions; otherwise iniquity will be your ruin. Cast away from you all the transgressions that you have committed against me, and get yourselves a new heart and a new spirit! Why will you die, O house of Israel? For I have no pleasure in the death of anyone, says the Lord GOD. Turn, then, and live. (Ezekiel 18:30-32)

God is the Great Shepherd. May we all accept the challenge to heed God's word for us, whether a word of challenge that we are prone to ignore, or a word of comfort and inspiration of which we are in need. May we be bold to accept our responsibilities, to take up our crosses, to turn to our God. May we be willing, not resistant, to hear God's call on our lives so that God, like a shepherd, can lead us with tender care, creating in us new hearts and bringing our dry bones to life.

CHAPTER 9

Bartholomew and the Oobleck

"The greatest among you will be your servant.
All who exalt themselves will be humbled, and
all who humble themselves will be exalted."
(Matthew 23:11-12)

"For if you forgive others their trespasses, your
heavenly Father will also forgive you; but if you
do not forgive others, neither will your Father
forgive your trespasses." (Matthew 6:14-15)

One of the most memorable episodes of the classic sitcom
Happy Days is the one in which "the Fonz," who is the
essence of coolness and self-confidence, makes a mistake and has
to admit it. Three or four times he tries to say, "I was wrong."
At first, all the further he can get out is, "I was wr——." He
struggles mightily to bring himself to acknowledge his error.

Bartholomew and the Oobleck is a story about a king, King
Derwin of the Kingdom of Didd, who has the same problem as
the Fonz. In addition to having trouble admitting he was wrong,
the king has a bit of trouble being content with what he has. It
seems that he has grown angry with, of all things, the sky.

Every year in the spring the sky produced rain. In the summer

60

it sent down sunshine. In the autumn it made fog, and in the winter, of course, snow. But these four had lost their luster for the king. In fact, he was bored with them. He wanted something new. Bartholomew tried to tell the king that, powerful though he was, the sky was one thing he could not rule.

But the king would not take no for an answer. He called on his magicians to get to work on the problem. Against Bartholomew's advice, the magicians promised the king that the next day he would have his wish. It would come in the form of a substance called "oobleck."

Sure enough, as promised, the next morning the king awakens to the sight of little green sputters of oobleck raining down from above. He is elated. He decides to declare this day a holiday. He orders the bell ringer to ring the bell. But the bell won't ring, because it's covered with the sticky green stuff. And a robin is stuck to her nest. The trumpeter tries to sound an alarm, but his trumpet gets clogged up with oobleck.

You get the picture. The oobleck sounded like a good idea, but soon it caused a lot more trouble than it was worth. The oobleck quite literally gums up the works of the entire Kingdom of Didd. Cooks can't cook; fiddlers can't fiddle; no one can do anything. Everyone, including the king, is stuck. And the oobleck keeps coming, unabated.

The wise Bartholomew tells the king that he can end this whole disaster by saying two simple words: "I'm sorry." But the king, like the Fonz, can't do it. He is too mighty, too proud to admit that he was wrong.

Bartholomew looks him straight in the eye and says, "You may be a mighty king. But you're sitting in oobleck up to your chin. And so is everyone else in your land. And if you won't even say you're sorry, *you're no sort of a king at all!*"

Finally, the king acknowledges that Bartholomew is right.

Reduced to sobbing, the king says the magic words. The oobleck disappears, and all is well with the kingdom again. All of a sudden, rain, sun, fog, and snow don't seem so bad anymore.

King Derwin of Didd is fictional, but his inability to say "I'm sorry" is all too real. In fact, for those of us in the non-fictional world, those two short words can be among the hardest words in the English language to say. They're not so hard to say if the offense is fairly minor or trivial—we were late for an appointment or we accidentally stepped on someone's toe while waiting in line. "Sorry," we say, and a minute later it's forgotten. But what about the father who comes to the realization that many of the problems of his adult children are the result of his having been too busy to spend time with them when they needed him most? What about the mother who for years has emotionally abused her children? What about the long-time friend who, in a moment of weakness or bad judgment, betrays a trust?

The king is far from alone. Once during a children's sermon, the leader asked, "What is the Bible about?" A child responded, "It's all about good people." Not really. In fact, throughout most of the Bible we encounter people who were not so good, who made mistakes and errors in judgment, who gave in to temptation, who surrendered to the lust for power. It started way back with Adam, and it included others who are regarded as heroes of faith: Jacob, Moses, David, and Paul. At some point, in order to move on, all of these—and many others—had to summon the humility and the courage to say the magic words: "I'm sorry." Whether that person was a king or not didn't matter.

The physical act of saying these words is simple. It takes about one second. It's not a tongue twister; it's easy to pronounce. The true difficulty in saying them lies in what they represent. These words, by their very nature, are self-effacing. The person who says them, and means them, has put himself or herself in a position of vulnerability and humility.

Yet the potential positive outcomes of saying "I'm sorry" can be profound. In Dr. Seuss's story, these two words saved the entire Kingdom of Didd. In our world, these words have the power to save and heal marriages, friendships, and families.

The wonderful power in these three syllables is found in what they represent: a turnaround, a new direction, a change of heart, a realization, sorrow, regret, compassion. Indeed, these two words signify new life, new hope, a fresh start. Where would we be without them? Where would we be if every mistake that we made meant the end? If every time we hurt another person, there was no way to get past the hurt and move on? Viewed in this light, the words "I'm sorry" are, ultimately, wonderful words of life. Those of us who are not capable of saying them are missing out on the key to overcoming our shortcomings and frailties—our sinful nature—in order to live anew.

We must remember, however, that the full potential of the words "I'm sorry" is influenced in part by the person who is hearing them. It's one thing to say "I'm sorry"; it's another thing to hear and accept those words. As hard as it is to say "I'm sorry," it can be even harder to say "I forgive you." Without forgiveness, "I'm sorry" remains suspended, waiting for a response that reestablishes the connection, that fixes what was broken.

The Bible tells us that those who do not know how to forgive will not be forgiven. At first glance, not receiving forgiveness appears to be a consequence—a divine punishment, if you will—for not offering forgiveness. Sometimes I wonder, however, if this is not so much a punishment as it is a true statement of spiritual and emotional reality. That is, perhaps it is not possible for someone who does not know how to forgive others to truly experience the freeing power that comes from being forgiven.

Forgiveness is, at its heart, an act of freedom. It grants the authority to another person to move on without being bound by past failures. But in forgiving, we not only free others, but also we free ourselves to live on. If saying "I'm sorry" requires practice and spiritual maturity, saying "I forgive you" takes even more practice and maturity.

We've all heard the expression "I can forgive, but I can never forget." I believe that as long as a person holds to that, he or she has not truly forgiven. Or at least such person has not yet experienced the full freeing power of forgiveness. A person who cannot forget is still living in the past, still unable to "let it go" and move on.

I am intrigued by the mystery of the human spirit, which is capable of both wonderful good and horrendous evil. This is true not just of the human race as a whole, but also of individual human beings. Within each and every one of us, the daily struggle to do right instead of wrong goes on. We are good and bad simultaneously. We believe by faith that we are made perfect in Christ, and yet we know all too well that our attitudes, thoughts, and behaviors are anything but perfect.

Still, we are on a path, a path known by some theological traditions as sanctification. We are not perfect, but we are striving for perfection, for spiritual maturity. As we strive, we are being shaped by the Author of perfection.

In this battle, as we put on the armor of the Lord, the words "I'm sorry" need to be at the forefront of our arsenal. We need to practice saying them with the confidence that, as with anything else, practice will make us better at it. After all, if the Fonz had had a little experience saying he was wrong, it wouldn't have been so hard for him to admit his error when he knew he finally had to.

The child who said that the Bible was all about good people didn't quite get it right, but that young sage wasn't altogether wrong either. The Bible is about one good person, someone who came to earth and died for the sins of humanity in order to free us to make use of the option of saying "I'm sorry." Without the hope of being freed from our sinful human nature, there would be no point in saying these words. We would be stuck, surrounded by oobleck.

"I'm sorry." These are freeing words, as are the words "I forgive you." And if both King Derwin of Didd and the Fonz could learn to say them, so can we.

CHAPTER 10

The Sneetches

There is no longer Jew or Greek, there is no longer slave or free, there is no longer male and female; for all of you are one in Christ Jesus. (Galatians 3:28)

My brothers and sisters, do you with your acts of favoritism really believe in our glorious Lord Jesus Christ? For if a person with gold rings and in fine clothes comes into your assembly, and if a poor person in dirty clothes also comes in, and if you take notice of the one wearing the fine clothes and say, "Have a seat here, please," while to the one who is poor you say, "Stand there," or, "Sit at my feet," have you not made distinctions among yourselves and become judges with evil thoughts?" (James 2:1-4)

Now, the Star-Belly Sneetches
Had bellies with stars.
The Plain-Belly Sneetches
Had none upon thars....
When the Star-Belly children went out to play ball,

Could a Plain Belly get in the game…? Not at all.
You only could play if your bellies had stars,
And the Plain Belly children had none upon thars.

The Sneetches in this Dr. Seuss story were, quite obviously, a divided society. Those with stars on their bellies thought that they were better than the Plain-Belly Sneetches. They never invited the Plain-Bellies to picnics or parties. Their children wouldn't play or talk with the other type of Sneetch.

Not only did the Star-Belly Sneetches think that they were better than the Plain-Bellies, but also—and this perhaps was the greater tragedy—the Plain-Belly Sneetches thought so too. They were not content to be treated differently, to be shunned, but at some level they accepted their inferiority instead of rejecting the second-rate label placed upon them. Although they were despised by Star-Belly Sneetches, they wanted to become them.

Then one day, someone comes to town who can give the Plain-Bellies a ray of hope. It seems that Sylvester McMonkey McBean has heard of their troubles and has invented a machine to fix them. All the Plain-Bellies had to do was walk through McBean's machine—after paying a small fee—and it would put a star on their tummies, making them look just like the Star-Bellies.

Lo and behold, the machine works! And for the first time in a long time, the formerly Plain-Belly Sneetches have smiles on their faces. Everyone is the same. Nobody, on the surface at least, is better than anyone else.

This, however, presents a problem for the original Star-Bellies. After all, they kind of liked things the way they were before. Like Yertle the Turtle, whom we met in an earlier chapter, they liked being king of the hill and looking down on other Sneetches. But fortunately for them—or so it seemed—Sylvester McMonkey McBean also has a machine to fix their problem. This machine works by removing—for a fee, of course—the stars from Sneetches' bellies. Now, the original Star-Bellies become plain. But at least they're distinguishable again from the other group of Sneetches, and, of course, they are better.

The Sneetches with stars respond by having their stars removed—again for a small fee. And those without stars have them put back on. And on and on it goes until everyone is unhappy with the vicious cycle that has been created—everyone except Sylvester McMonkey McBean, who skips town with a boatload full of money, two slick machines, and a sly, victorious smile.

This story is rich with social commentary about how fallen human beings search for ways to make divisions among themselves. It also makes a statement about those who have a vested interest in keeping people divided and at war because they can sell their product to both sides.

There is nothing inherently better about having a star or not having one. After all, the Star-Bellies are more than willing to have their stars removed if it will make them different again. Thus, the perception that one appearance is better than the other is just that: perception, not reality.

Our world has a lot to learn from the Sneetches. We are far more prone to dwell on our differences than we are to celebrate and build upon our common humanity. We stereotype people who look, think, act, or believe a certain way. We form prejudices and make jokes about people based on the clothes they wear or what neighborhood they come from.

Our "race-related" prejudices linger even in the face of hard scientific evidence to the contrary. Geneticists tell us that people of every ethnic background are so overwhelmingly similar genetically that it makes no sense even to use the term "race" in describing our differences: humankind is comprised of just one race.

The church of Jesus Christ has an opportunity to model unity for the world, but unfortunately his followers sometimes are part of the problem. This is nothing new. In the passage that opens this chapter, Paul is writing to churches in Galatia, Asia Minor. In these churches there were those who came from a Jewish heritage and those who came from a Gentile background. Was one superior to the other? Paul writes,

> Just as Abraham "believed God, and it was reckoned to him as righteousness," so, you see, those who believe are the descendants of Abraham. And the scripture, foreseeing that God would justify the Gentiles by faith, declared the gospel beforehand to Abraham, saying, "All the Gentiles shall be blessed in you." For this reason, those who believe are blessed with Abraham who believed. (Galatians 3:6-9)

The church has something to learn from an unusual source: the 1979 Pittsburgh Pirates baseball team. The team's much publicized theme song that year, in which they won the World Series, was Sister Sledge's "We Are Family." Indeed, in Jesus Christ, the church is one big family. There are no Star-Belly or Plain-Belly Christians. The church is comprised of people of different ethnic backgrounds, different economic classes, and different age groups. Our challenge, and our opportunity, is to use these differences to enrich the church instead of allowing them to divide us.

As a pastor, I sometimes witnessed division between longtime members and newcomers. It's easy for some longtime members to think of themselves as "true Christians." They view new members with suspicion until the latter prove themselves. I know of one church in which members had yet to truly put the Civil War behind them. Folks originally from the North and others from the South did not truly recognize each other as brothers and sisters in Christ. Different cultural assumptions created friction: true Southerners versus carpetbaggers. It was Galatia all over again. And in this setting, the words from James 2:1-4 regarding favoritism seemed foreign.

Many times the superior/inferior games that we play, even in the church, are a bit more subtle, but nonetheless are attempts to put "stars upon thars." John Wesley spoke of the catholic spirit: "If your heart is with my heart, give me your hand." It is with this attitude that we in the church must accept one another as God accepts us. The traditional custom of calling others "brothers" and "sisters" is a healthy one. We are family. We all have different gifts, and we all need each other, just as each part of the body depends on the other parts in order for the whole to function at its best.

So often, the things that divide are trivial things, not much different from stars upon bellies. We who are Christians need to recognize and appreciate more fully the family traits that unite us:

■ *Creation.* We all are created by God. We are both alike and different from one another, but God called the whole of creation good.

■ *Calling.* There is purpose in life for each and every one of us. Just as the prophets in the Old Testament were called, we too are called for a purpose.

■ *Sin.* All of us have fallen short of what God requires. We deceive ourselves if we think we have not sinned. But to acknowledge this does not mean accepting it as the last word.

■ *Christ.* We share in the grace of our Lord Jesus Christ. God loves us despite our failings. This is by far the most important basis for our unity.

Proclaiming and celebrating unity in the church means learning from our differences instead of allowing them to divide us. It means encouraging others and not boasting about our own accomplishments. It means courting a spirit of gratitude instead of pride. It means that we cannot separate love for God from love for one another.

The story of the Sneetches has a happy ending. They lost all their money, and perhaps that's what it took for them finally to realize something far more important than money. They realized that a Sneetch was a Sneetch, whether Star-Bellied or not.

No kind of Christian is the best Christian in the church. There are no Star-Belly Christians. We are family. We are one in Jesus Christ.

CHAPTER 11

The Butter Battle Book

"You have heard that it was said, 'An eye for an eye and a tooth for a tooth.' But I say to you, Do not resist an evildoer. But if anyone strikes you on the right cheek, turn the other also...." (Matthew 5:38-39)

Love is patient; love is kind; love is not envious or boastful or arrogant or rude. It does not insist on its own way; it is not irritable or resentful; it does not rejoice in wrongdoing, but rejoices in the truth. It bears all things, believes all things, hopes all things, endures all things. (1 Corinthians 13:4-7)

D r. Seuss's *The Butter Battle Book* was written early in the 1980s, a peak time of concern about nuclear proliferation, particularly in the United States and what was then the Soviet Union. It is perhaps the author's most direct venture into social commentary.

The story focuses on a long-standing battle between the Yooks, who live on one side of a dividing wall, and the Zooks, who live on the other side. The grandfather of a young boy in the story decides that it's time to tell his grandson about the ongoing feud between his people, the Yooks, and those horrible Zooks on the other side of the wall. He discloses to his grandson the horrible truth that when Zooks eat bread, they do so with the buttered side down, instead of the correct way—the Yooks' way—buttered side up.

Physical confrontation between the disputing sides begins with a slingshot, but soon it escalates into bigger weapons capable of far more destruction. The grandfather is appointed to head the military effort against the Zooks, with the Yooks' leader guaranteeing that the needed ammunition will be provided.

The weapons keep getting bigger and bigger. But each time the grandfather goes to the wall, it seems that his counterpart on the other side of the wall, VanItch, returns with an even more daunting weapon aimed in the Yooks' direction. When the grandfather returns from the wall, each time he is assured by the Yook leader that the Yooks are on the winning side:

> "My Boys in the Back Room have finally found how.
> Just wait till you see what they've puttered up now!
> In their great new machine you'll fly over that Wall
> and clobber those Butter-Down Zooks one and all!"

Confident, he returns to the wall, only to find:

> "VanItch had a Sputter exactly like mine!
> And he yelled, 'My Blue-Gooer is working just fine!
> And I'm here to say that if Yooks can goo Zooks,
> you'd better forget it. 'Cause Zooks can goo Yooks!'"

Finally, the grandfather receives the ultimate weapon, the Bitsy Big-Boy Boomeroo. It's so small that it can be held between two fingers of one hand, but it's capable of doing such massive destruction that all Yooks are ordered to live underground in a big hole for the time being.

When the grandfather takes his place on the wall, who is there brandishing the same weapon but his nemesis, VanItch! The story ends with the two enemies standing atop the wall, each holding the ultimate weapon of mass destruction, staring at the other, and fearfully wondering who will go first. This tense, foreboding ending captures the essence of the message of those who opposed policies that critics of the time referred to collectively as MAD ("mutually assured destruction").

This somewhat depressing story is partly a commentary on "powers and principalities." Sometimes institutions, though established by human beings, take on a life of their own, adopting a power and momentum that make them difficult to control. But in acknowledging this message, we should not miss what this cautionary tale about Yooks and Zooks has to teach us about human nature.

Specifically, it appears to be inherent in sinful human nature to see reality—to view the world—from a selfish perspective. This tendency is readily apparent in athletic contests. Go to a sporting event at any level from junior high school up through the pros, and you will find two opponents who don't necessarily like the other side. You will also find referees or umpires who don't have a "rooting" interest but whose job it is to make sure that both sides are treated fairly. At almost any game, fans (including parents) of both sides will agree on one thing: "The refereeing wasn't fair. The ref favored the other team. Our side was cheated."

This is the case even if the official is completely fair. It's human nature to see things from our own selfish perspective, and thus to emphasize the questionable calls that went against our team and not those that went in our favor.

The same is true to some extent of journalists. A journalist is a referee of sorts, an arbiter who is charged with the difficult responsibility of telling both sides of a controversial story fairly and impartially, only to be regularly accused of favoring one side or the other.

"It's not fair" is one of the most heavily used and whiny childhood laments. One child does something to another, and the second child does something to get even. But "getting even," in light of this inherently selfish perspective, usually means giving back a little more than we got. So when one child hits another, the second child hits back just a little harder. Seeing that as unfair, the first hits harder yet, and on and on it goes.

The Old Testament admonition of "an eye for an eye and a tooth for a tooth" was the ideal. But at least it could serve to limit the escalation that inevitably results from inherently selfish human nature, which tends to want to take two teeth for every tooth the other person took from us.

"An eye for an eye and a tooth for a tooth" thus was a step in the right direction, intended to limit the damage, to stop the madness of the natural process of escalation. But Jesus offered an even better way: "Do not resist an evildoer."

To be sure, various commentators have pointed out that this verse, once the whole cultural context is understood, is not intended to advocate the idea of believers allowing others to run roughshod over them. Yet clearly it is an admonition to halt the violence, to stop the escalation.

What does it take to follow a different path, a different way? What must we do to begin to address and overcome our selfish human nature? I believe that it begins with an intentional effort to get "outside ourselves" in an effort to understand life in general and particular situations from another person's perspective. What if the Yooks and the Zooks had sat down and talked about their differences in an effort to understand one another's position? Might it have made a difference?

Many of our conflicts, whether international, national, community, or familial, can be addressed simply by both sides understanding each other. One common exercise in marriage counseling is to have one spouse repeat the message being delivered by the other spouse—not interpret or analyze or respond to it, but simply repeat it, just to make sure that the one clearly understands what the other is saying. We would all be surprised at the number of times in these settings that one says to the other, "No, that's not what I was saying at all." And that's when progress begins, with a more careful effort to listen to and truly understand another's perspective.

We can apply the principle of this exercise to conflicts of all kinds. It does not necessarily mean that the problem will be solved. For it is entirely possible that once two parties who are at odds understand the other accurately and completely, they will remain at odds. Perhaps they have different values or interpretations. But many conflicts can be resolved simply as a result of people understanding other people and recognizing, even in the midst of disagreement, other perspectives.

To listen carefully in an effort to understand another constitutes the essence of love, which requires both patience and kindness. Who are the Zooks in our Yookish lives? Will we hit them back, or will we try to understand them? One way offers the potential to resolve our differences. The other way leads us down the path of hitting harder and harder.

CHAPTER 12

The Grinch (Again)

"Pray then in this way:
Our Father in heaven,
hallowed be your name.
Your kingdom come.
Your will be done,
on earth as it is in heaven.
Give us this day our daily bread."
(Matthew 6:9-11)

The most obvious and basic lesson of Dr. Seuss's *How the Grinch Stole Christmas!* speaks to the issue of the priorities in our lives. What gets the most attention? The most time? The most energy? Is it things or is it people? Are we more concerned about owning or being? About making more money or growing closer to other people and to God?

We routinely hear various commentators, including religious commentators, expound on what has gone wrong with our society. They blame various factors, including the decline of family values, the entertainment industry, the media, and the banning of organized prayer from public schools. In the midst of this kind of analysis, it seems that the negative influences of materialism rarely get their proper due.

Simply put, we live in a materialistic culture, defined in terms of "busyness," a society that is much more interested in material things than spiritual things. As a society, we are captive to our seemingly unquenchable thirst for more. Advertisements suggest to us, in both subtle and not-so-subtle ways, that we are not really living if we don't drive a certain kind of car or wear a particular brand of clothes.

We have mistakenly equated the acquisition of possessions with happiness and fulfillment. We need to listen to the words of the many people who testify that they feel they had more back in the days when they had less—more happiness, that is, even when there was less money and fewer things.

People who want to defend a materialistic lifestyle are quick to point out that it is not money that lies at the root of all evil, but rather the love of money. True though this is, this defense typically is offered as a way to avoid confronting the issue of materialism. After all, if "love" is defined in terms of where we spend our most valued time and energy, then it is easily argued that our culture, as a whole, indeed does love money, as do many who are a part of the culture.

Money—material things—cannot produce happiness. In fact, many a lottery winner has testified that sudden fortune, despite the initial appeal, has not ultimately improved their quality of life. Often, it makes life worse. For one thing, the newly wealthy person might have trouble determining who his or her friends really are.

Recently, I heard a couple talking about the time when their family income was $25,000. They thought that if they could only get it up to $40,000, they would have everything they ever wanted. But a few years later, when their income had reached the $40,000 mark, they started saying that they needed $50,000 to solve all their financial problems. Today, their income is over

$70,000, and they still have bills that they are not always able to pay, and things that they want but cannot afford.

It seems that no matter what people have, whether a little or a lot, they all want the same thing: more. Again, this would not be a problem if we were satisfied when we got the "more" that we wanted. But the problem with human nature is that, short of a spirituality that ultimately rejects materialism, more seems to be never enough.

A fascination with material things has reordered our culture's values and priorities in harmful ways. It has contributed to a greater division between rich and poor, in contrast to a society in which all feel welcome and equally represented.

As we have accumulated more and more things, we, as a culture, have become more and more independent and ostensibly self-sufficient. We have abandoned the front porches that used to serve as gathering places for neighbors, and we have picked up the remote control for our garage door so we can get into the house without having to see, let alone speak with, a neighbor.

Even though we occasionally give it lip service, we have failed to heed the maxim "Money cannot buy happiness." We need to understand that the big-screen TV or the shiny sportscar can provide a temporary burst of joy, just as a ball of newspaper tossed on a campfire makes it flare up. But if there are no hot embers lying beneath the flames, the fire dies out quickly.

Not only is it true that things cannot produce happiness, but also there is plenty of reason to believe that things can actually stand in the way of ultimate happiness. They provide the illusion of contentment while preventing us from exploring the relationships and making the emotional and spiritual connections required to produce true and lasting joy. Thus, things produce the expectation of happiness, only to let us down.

In recognition of this reality, when Jesus modeled prayer for his disciples, he prayed, "Give us this day our daily bread." He didn't ask for a five-course, soup-to-nuts dinner! And so we should pray in the same spirit, asking for daily bread, not a luxurious limousine or a gigantic home-entertainment theater. No "name it and claim it" here—just the basic necessities to live another day so that we can focus on the truly important things in life.

This is something that the Grinch didn't understand—not at first, anyway. He thought that if he could just take all the things away from the *Whos*—their toys and their tricycles and their pudding and roast beast—he could take away their happiness and make them angry and miserable.

When the *Whos* woke up on Christmas morning, they didn't even have their "daily bread," for the Grinch had taken every last morsel of food from *Who*-ville. Pleased with his night's work, the Grinch figured that all those *Whos* were in for a big surprise.

But it was the Grinch who was in for the surprise. For instead of crying or wailing, the *Whos* never missed a beat. The fact that they were missing all their presents and trimmings and food didn't faze them one bit. This is quite the contrast from some families I'm sure we all know, whose children have been known to leave the room bawling if they didn't get every last thing on their Christmas list. (Of course, *our* children would never behave that way!)

All those things that the Grinch had taken were accoutrements, mere symbols of the more important and lasting values that the *Whos* held dear. And so the *Whos* formed a big circle and held hands. Young and old, male and female, they joined together in song, celebrating life and love, family and friends. Nothing that was truly important to them was missing on that Christmas morning; everything that was important was present.

It was this tacit but visible rejection of materialistic values that ultimately enabled the Grinch to draw closer to a truer understanding of the importance of Christmas:

> "Maybe Christmas," he thought, "*doesn't* come
> from a store.
> "Maybe Christmas…perhaps…means a little bit more!"

And it was this understanding that enabled the Grinch's undersized heart to grow three sizes. Christmas does mean a little more. In fact, it means a lot more. The Savior of the world came into that world born of a poor, humble virgin who came to town on a donkey. He spent his first night in a barn among the animals. In such humble places, not in the things of this world, can be found the keys to true and lasting joy.

CHAPTER 13

On Beyond Zebra!

After these things God tested Abraham. He said to him, "Abraham!" And he said, "Here I am." He said, "Take your son, your only son Isaac, whom you love, and go to the land of Moriah, and offer him there as a burnt offering on one of the mountains that I shall show you." So Abraham rose early in the morning, saddled his donkey, and took two of his young men with him, and his son Isaac; he cut the wood for the burnt offering, and set out and went to the place in the distance that God had shown him. On the third day Abraham looked up and saw the place far away. Then Abraham said to his young men, "Stay here with the donkey; the boy and I will go over there; we will worship, and then we will come back to you." Abraham took the wood of the burnt offering and laid it on his son Isaac, and he himself carried the fire and the knife. So the two of them walked on together. Isaac said to his father Abraham, "Father!" And he said, "Here I am, my son." He said, "The fire and the wood are here, but where is the lamb for a burnt offering?" Abraham said, "God himself will provide the lamb for a burnt offering, my son." So the two of them walked on together....

The angel of the LORD called to Abraham a second time from heaven, and said, "By myself I have sworn, says the LORD: Because you have done this, and have not withheld your son, your only son, I will indeed bless you, and I will make your offspring as numerous as the stars of heaven and as the sand that is on the seashore. And your offspring shall possess the gate of their enemies, and by your offspring shall the nations of the earth gain blessing for themselves, because you have obeyed my voice." (Genesis 22:1-8,15-18)

The Dr. Seuss story *On Beyond Zebra!* prompts us to imagine life beyond the boundaries that others have placed on us or beyond boundaries that perhaps *we* have placed on ourselves. Most people confine the English alphabet to twenty-six letters, with Z inevitably standing for "Zebra." But not the person who was teaching Conrad O'Dell to spell:

Said Conrad Cornelius O'Donald O'Dell,
My very young friend who is learning to spell:
"The A is for Ape. And the B is for Bear.
"The C is for Camel. The H is for Hare.
"The M is for Mouse. And the R is for Rat.
"I know *all* the twenty-six letters like that...."
And I said, "You can stop, if you want, with the Z
"Because most people stop with the Z
"*But not me!*"

The teacher then goes on to introduce little Conrad to a whole new world that he'd never imagined before. He introduces letters such as Glikk and Snee and Thnad, and characters such as Sneedles and Nutches and Floob-Boober-Bab-Boober-Bubs.

What happens when we go "on beyond Zebra" either by our own choice or as a result of the circumstances we face in life? Going on beyond Zebra can mean discovering new insights, meeting new people, considering new ideas, finding renewed faith, venturing out beyond our comfort zones, or summoning resources that we may not have known we had.

Abraham was challenged by God more than once to go on beyond Zebra. He was, no doubt, a bright enough fellow, but he was also cautious. And he was pushed beyond the comfortable boundaries imposed by his cautious approach when he was called to leave his homeland and travel hundreds of miles across the desert. He had to abandon much in order to be the father of a great people. A reasonable person, he was pushed beyond reason when, as a toothless old man, he and his aged wife, Sarah, were told that they were to have a child to fulfill the promise of the Lord. Sarah laughed, but Abraham trusted. And Isaac, whose name means "laughter," was born.

Now a family man, Abraham loved his wife dearly. And Isaac was his beloved, promised child. Abraham's love for him was immense, but now he was being pushed again, pushed beyond even family bonds. It had been hard wandering across the desert, leaving everything behind. It had been hard waiting for a promised child while growing old and gray. But now this child, this beloved Isaac, is required by God as a sacrifice, appearing to make God's previous promise null and void.

Abraham's heart was torn. What could be worse than to hear the voice of God asking you to kill your child? This was the same voice that Abraham had followed across desert wastelands. It was the same voice he had followed and trusted while waiting for the child to be born. Now he had to choose between sacrificing his son Isaac upon the mountain or denying his God. Abraham got up, took Isaac, the firewood, and the knife. He set out to do what he had heard God tell him to do.

Isaac knew that something was amiss. He asked, "Dad, where's the lamb for slaughter?" Tears came to Abraham's eyes as he replied, "Surely, the Lord will provide." He arranged the firewood. An altar place was prepared. The moment of truth had arrived. Binding his own son, Abraham prepared for the very worst. And then, suddenly, he heard the voice of the Lord's angel telling him that Isaac was not to be sacrificed after all. And then he spotted a ram caught in the bushes. God provided.

And the voice said that it was good that Abraham was willing to relinquish even his precious one. It was good that Abraham held on to his trust in God even when he was confused and torn between family and God. Isaac was the only heir of Abraham, and the only way that God's promise of descendants as numerous as grains of sand by the sea could be fulfilled. Abraham showed that he was willing to go beyond Zebra—beyond comfort, beyond reason, beyond familiar bounds—trusting that the promise of God would never fail, because his God, our God, is faithful.

The story is told that near the end of the Twelfth Century there was a young man whose father was a cloth merchant. The young man loved to ride up and down the road on his fine steed. He loved the horse almost as much as he loved a good party with wine, women, and song. He had a great time night after night. If he lived today, we would find him at one of the local community watering holes as he moved from one establishment to the next in pursuit of a few tall ones.

Yes, he had a great time. As he rode his horse, he saw beggars on the street. He would flip a beggar a coin, as was the custom of the day. He did it in part because he cared, but mostly to show that he had what the beggar did not. One day as he was riding along, he saw a man who'd been completely disfigured by leprosy. He flipped him a coin in his customary arrogant manner and kept riding by. But suddenly something on beyond Zebra got ahold of him. He stopped, dismounted, and went back to the man. He gave him more gold and embraced him.

From that day on, the young man began to look differently at people whom society considered "the least." He noticed them, cared for them, and devoted his life to them. Time and time again, he cared for people in need. Once, he fixed a church building that had fallen into disrepair. His father said to him, "Son, I don't understand why you are hanging out with these low-class people. I want you to be in the cloth business, take care of everything for me, and handle my fortune. But if you keep this up, I'll have to disinherit you."

The young man stripped off all his clothes except for some underclothing and said, "Then I guess I'm no longer your son. I have to follow my Lord." And so the man whom we call Francis of Assisi continued his compassionate work, taking up a life of caring for the least of God's children. It has been said that he redeemed the church in a time when it had become little more than a cold institution. He brought life and love back to the church in his simple way. He went on beyond Zebra, beyond what could be expected. He trusted God.

It was about 1960 when Millard Fuller made his first million dollars. It began when he was a student at the University of Alabama. He and a friend had opened a printing company, Fuller and Dees. They printed and sold cookbooks. During college, he made a tremendous amount of money. Following college, he went to law school. He and his partner moved to Montgomery, Alabama. One day the accountant called and said, "I have some news for you. According to my records, you are now a millionaire. What's next?" Millard replied, "On to ten million, on to a hundred million."

For Millard, however, things were not right at home. Some of the values that he had held when he was younger—when he and his wife, Linda, had first met and made a covenant to love each other and to love God—had gotten displaced along the way. Finally, she left him. She went to New York, called home, and said that she needed some time away, but that he could come to see her if he wanted to in about a week's time. He went to New York to see what was left to salvage from their relationship. The two went to see the Broadway play *It's Never Too Late*. They came out and were going to take a taxi ride through Central Park. When they opened the taxi door, the driver said, "Congratulations, this is your lucky day. You are the first ones to ride in my new taxicab."

They took it as a sign that maybe there was a chance for new life for them. They took long walks, sat on the steps of a cathedral, and talked and talked about what had gone wrong in their life together and why things weren't like they wanted them to be. Finally, they came to the conclusion that they had to return to the Christian faith that had been so important to them in earlier years. They chose to go on beyond Zebra, opting to explore new territory outside their comfort zones.

After a few phone calls, Millard Fuller had his accountant busy working at giving away his wealth. Millard gave it away to charitable institutions of one kind or another. He and Linda moved to a Christian community at Americus, Georgia. From there, they became involved in fixing up homes for people living in poverty in that area. Fuller took all the brilliance and insights that had helped him amass his fortune and put them to work building homes. In 1964 he began what is now Habitat for Humanity, an organization that over the last four decades has built over one hundred thousand homes in the United States and in countries all over the world. "Simple Jesus economics" is what they call it: people working together to provide a decent home for all God's people. And it has happened because Millard and Linda Fuller were willing to go on beyond Zebra, beyond what most people consider normal and reasonable.

Jean Vanier is yet another example of someone who went on beyond Zebra. He was a Canadian naval officer. Upon leaving the navy, he did the unexpected. His father had been a political leader in Canada, but Jean took a different route. Buying a home north of Paris, he invited Raphael and Philippe, two men with mental disabilities, to live with him. Someone asked, "Why are you doing that?" Jean replied, "I think it is what Jesus wants me to do." The two men moved in with him, and they found that as a family, a community, they could live together.

This was a new way of treating people with disabilities. When such people are placed into or remain in family units, they can have more viable, fulfilling lives. Jean Vanier's action began L'Arche (named after Noah's ark). This organization now has over 120 communities in thirty countries, all because Jean Vanier was willing to go beyond Zebra, beyond what is normally expected in life.

Most of those who go on beyond Zebra are not famous or internationally known. The world has never heard of a dear friend of mine, Faye Pickel. After she retired from a mission that she had served for many years, everyone thought that Faye would go back home to Tennessee and sit in a rocking chair. Instead, she went to Tifton, Georgia, and in retirement she played the piano for two churches, one on Sunday morning and another on Wednesday nights. She also got very involved in church ministry. Faye could have said, "It's time to retire and take it easy." Instead, she went on beyond Zebra in living out a simple, serving faith.

In Jerusalem many years ago, a small band of close friends finished a meal at which emotions ran high. Their leader—our Savior—had shared food and drink and spoken of his body and blood. He had wrapped a towel around his waist and washed their feet. Although they were very close friends, someone spoke of betrayal. And in that intimate setting, they looked at each other and said, "Lord, is it I? Is it I?" A few of them, those especially close to him, went out with him to a garden to pray. Jesus continued to pray and struggle even after his friends fell asleep. He was a long way from Nazareth, a long way from Galilee, a long way from those walks on the beach and the joyful times they had spent together healing and teaching and feeding.

The events that lay ahead were all too clear to him. He could see the cross before him: "Father, I don't want to do this, but nevertheless, not my will but yours be done." And he prayed and struggled. He was in such distress that drops of sweat, then drops of blood, formed upon his brow. But he went forward—on beyond Zebra—trusting in God. On he went to the cross of death, and later to the empty tomb of resurrection. We have this same opportunity to press on ahead, following the path of faith in spite of what we can see or neatly reason out.

Several years ago a group of students from various denominational backgrounds got together to discuss the question "What are the minimal requirements for a being a Christian?" This entailed asking questions such as "What do you have to believe?" "How do you have to be baptized?" and "What do you have to do?" The discussion dragged on for a while, until one woman rose and headed for the door. The convener called her back and said, "Excuse me, where are you going? Don't you like our discussion?" She replied, "No, not really. I'm not interested in what is the least requirement to be a Christian. I came here trying to find out what's the most I can do for my Jesus."

That is the call for us. It should not be a question of what we need to do to get by, but rather of how much we can do for our Lord, who has done so much for us. This is the faith of Abraham, the faith of Francis of Assisi, the faith of Millard Fuller, Jean Vanier, and Faye Pickel. It is ultimately the faith we have in Jesus Christ that allows God to take us on beyond the expected to something greater still—beyond comfort, beyond family, beyond wealth, beyond age, beyond disability, even beyond death. May this faith inspire us each day to stretch beyond our limits, to care for those within the flock and to reach out to others, to reach beyond the status quo, to exceed normal expectations—on beyond Zebra, as far as our faith, love, and imaginations will allow.